Baseball Memories
1900-1909

Marc Okkonen

Sterling Publishing Co., Inc.   New York

Library of Congress Cataloging-in-Publication Data

Okkonen, Marc.
    Baseball memories : 1900–1909 / Marc Okkonen.
        p.   cm.
    Includes index.
    ISBN 0-8069-8728-6
    1. Baseball—United States—History—20th century. I. Title.
GV863.A1038   1992
796.357′0973—dc20   92–20532
                                                     CIP

10 9 8 7 6 5 4 3 2 1

Published by Sterling Publishing Company, Inc.
387 Park Avenue South, New York, N.Y. 10016
© 1992 by Marc Okkonen
Distributed in Canada by Sterling Publishing
℅ Canadian Manda Group, P.O. Box 920, Station U
Toronto, Ontario, Canada M8Z 5P9
Distributed in Great Britain and Europe by Cassell PLC
Villiers House, 41/47 Strand, London WC2N 5JE, England
Distributed in Australia by Capricorn Link Ltd.
P.O. Box 665, Lane Cove, NSW 2066
Printed and bound in Hong Kong
All rights reserved

Sterling   ISBN 0-8069-8728-6

Design & paste-up assembly:
    Marc Okkonen

Typesetting:
    Sharon Tingley

Photocopy work:
    COMPUTER CIRCUIT INC., Gardena, CA
    PROFESSIONAL COLOR SERVICE, Muskegon, MI
    BRIDGES NETWORK, Muskegon, MI

Photos xerographed from files of the
National Baseball Library, microfilm copies
of period newspapers and various
miscellaneous sources.

Original line art (locator maps, ballpark
drawings, and uniform illustrations)
copyrighted by the author.

Sources & Contributors:
    National Baseball Library, Cooperstown, NY
    Washington D.C. Public Library
    Library of Congress
    Carnegie Library of Pittsburgh, PA
    Enoch Pratt Free Library, Baltimore, MD
    Cleveland Public Library
    Cincinnati Public Library
    Milwaukee Public Library
    Historical Society of Washington D.C.
    AAF Library, Los Angeles
    Philadelphia Public Library
    Clarence Blasco
    Bob Davids
    Larry Gerlach
    Ed Koller
    Jack Lang
    Steven Mark
    Dick & Helen Miller
    Paul Pogharian
    Rich Tourengeau

DEDICATION

To the daily newspapers in the major league cities of the period, which provided a daily diary of baseball history...and especially to the baseball writers who provided eyewitness accounts and background information required for compiling much of this volume. And a special tribute to the photographers whose diligent works have preserved an accurate visual record of a memorable era in the history of the game.

TABLE OF CONTENTS

A DECADE TO REMEMBER

The decade that followed the opening of the twentieth century was filled with important events and developments that forever influenced the future course of American history. It was an age of phenomenal industrial growth fueled by wave after wave of immigrants from Europe who provided much of the needed labor force. It was also a decade of significant social reform and political change. America was emerging from the cocoon of isolationism to assume its destiny as a major world power. It was a time of judgment for the excesses of monopolistic capitalism. Important issues were debated everywhere during the decade—the rights of organized labor, prohibition of alcoholic beverages, pure food and drug laws, women's suffrage, child labor, conservation of natural resources, the gold standard, statehood for many western territories. The political star of the decade was the young, energetic president Theodore Roosevelt, whose bold initiatives mirrored the dynamic mood of the times. His successor, William Howard Taft, though decidedly less vigorous, closed out the decade and became the first U.S. President to preside over baseball's opener in Washington.

Wm. McKinley began the decade as U.S. President, but was cut down by an assassin's bullet in the fall of 1901. Vice President Theodore Roosevelt became the new Chief Executive and served through 1908.

U.S. population in 1900 stood at 76 million. The influx of immigrants over the next ten years totaled well over 8 million, swelling the 1910 census to 92 million, an astonishing increase of 21%. As the percentage of farm labor decreased in a burgeoning industrial climate, most of the population increase was absorbed in the large industrial cities in the northeast corner of the nation. This population trend had a significant impact on major league baseball, which by no coincidence also was encamped in the same industrial urban population centers.

Teddy Roosevelt advocated the rigors of outdoor life and athletic activities but never expressed any particular devotion to baseball.

Technological growth and important new inventions also played a major role in the reshaping of American life in the 1900-09 decade. Electric power and telephone service were well established in 1900 urban America and grew in leaps and bounds during the following ten years. Except for the electrically powered street car and railway systems, horses were the main ingredient of urban transportation as the decade began. But the contraption that had the most impact on big city transportation patterns, the automobile, was on the brink of popularity and affordability. By the end of the decade, the urban horse was well on its way to eventual extinction as the sight of increasing numbers of the noisy gas-buggies on city streets became commonplace by 1910. The railroads were still the principal means of long distance travel and they also enjoyed a decade of healthy growth and prosperity. The only threat to their monopoly was still far in the future as the decade saw the very first heavier-than-air flight by the Wright brothers at Kitty Hawk in 1903. Other important new developments during the decade that would alter future living patterns were the motion picture camera, finally patented by Edison in 1908, and primitive breakthroughs in wireless radio. Edison's talking machine was in popular use by 1900 and the new disk-type records were replacing wax cylinders in popularity. Telegraph and its stepchild, the teletype machine, were already in use and played a crucial role in the swift transmission of up-to-the-minute baseball news.

SOME POPULAR GADGETS OF 1900-1909

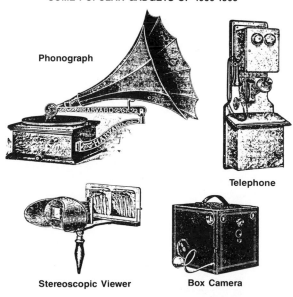

Phonograph

Telephone

Stereoscopic Viewer

Box Camera

President William Howard Taft, TR's successor, became baseball's most visible fan. Taft, unlike Teddy, enjoyed the National Pastime and used his honorary pass often to root for the hapless Washington nine. His presence at opening day established a permanent tradition.

Recreation hours for the average city worker were more limited for post-1900 America. The 10-hour day and 6-day workweek were common, leaving precious little time to escape from the tedium of routine labors. Sundays provided the only full day for many to attend church service and devote some time to more leisurely and pleasurable activities. A trip to the countryside or a picnic in the park were moments to be treasured by city folk. But the nation was still in the grip of religious puritanism and certain activities on the Sabbath were generally frowned upon, including baseball. Ironically, the one day of the week that provided baseball with its biggest potential audience was illegal in the majority of major league towns. That left only Saturday dates and summer holidays for attracting the sellout crowds necessary for a profitable baseball operation. Considering the effects of this damaging restriction, the steadily increasing attendance figures during the decade are indeed a testament to the popularity of the game.

The main competition for the public's recreational expenditures of 1900-09 came from vaudeville, plays, concerts, circuses, wild west shows, and nickelodeons which showcased that new-fangled attraction called the moving picture. The first full-length feature, Edison's "THE GREAT TRAIN ROBBERY," captivated a national audience. Popular idols of the day on the musical stage were Enrico Caruso, Sarah Bernhardt, and John Philip Sousa. Buffalo Bill Cody brought the thrills of frontier days to the Eastern big cities with his touring Wild West shows. Bicycling was both a popular leisure activity and fiercely contested form of racing. The America's Cup sailing races and automobile racing were also popular events—Sir Thomas Lipton and Barney Oldfield were household words. In boxing, Jim Jeffries retained the heavyweight championship in 1900 from Gentleman Jim Corbett (whose brother Joe was a major league baseball player). Jeffries retired in 1905 and the title went to Tommy Burns until Jack Johnson came along in 1908. Willie Anderson was the top golfer of the decade, winning the U.S. Open four times. Basketball was still in its infancy but collegiate football was a popular, though brutal, spectator sport. Football injuries were so commonplace that even President Roosevelt joined the call for reforms, which were introduced in 1905.

Lillian Russell drew star billing wherever she appeared.

Sarah Bernhardt was the most popular female stage personality of the decade.

John Philip Sousa, the march king, was at the height of his fame.

Barney Oldfield, the first big name in auto racing, helped popularize the automobile as a device for recreational pleasure.

Professional football had its roots in the early 1900's. Pictured here are the Philadelphia Athletics, managed by none other than baseball's Connie Mack (center).

The University of Michigan's "point-a-minute" gridders, under Fielding Yost, were the dominant collegiate eleven after the turn of the century. They defeated Stanford 49-0 in the first Rose Bowl game in January 1902.

Basketball was still in its embryonic stage in the post-1900 years. The open-bottom basket had not yet been adopted.

The Harvard-Yale game was already a heralded annual event by 1900. Note the many helmetless players.

Jack Johnson emerged late in the decade as the dominant heavyweight in boxing—one of the few major sports that were grudgingly open to blacks.

Fairs and exhibitions were another popular activity that attracted visitors by the millions. The first important such affair was the Pan-American exposition, which opened in Buffalo in 1901. It was a resounding success, but is best remembered for being the site of the tragic assassination of President William McKinley in September of that year. The best attended fair of the decade was the 1904 St. Louis World's Fair, which celebrated the centennial of the Louisiana Purchase. A feature of that fair that was almost lost among the numerous dazzling exhibits and sideshows was the third modern Olympic games, the first staged in the U.S.

Calamities and tragedies also marked the first decade of the new century. Galveston, Texas was heavily damaged with great loss of lives by storm and floods in 1900. Chelsea, Massachusetts was virtually loveled by fire later in the decade. Other devastating tragedies from fire were the ship General Slocum in New York in 1904 and the Iroquois Theater in Chicago in 1903 (Major Leaguers Charles Dexter and John Houseman were on the scene and saved many lives with heroic deeds). A series of deadly mine accidents made the news almost annually. But the most publicized natural disaster of the decade was the earthquake and subsequent fire that flattened San Francisco in April 1906. Besides McKinley, we lost two ex-presidents during the decade—Benjamin Harrison in 1901 and Grover Cleveland in 1908.

International events which made headlines at the turn of the century included the Boxer Rebellion in China, the Boer War in South Africa, and the Russo-Japanese war. Teddy Roosevelt enhanced his reputation as a statesman by arranging the Treaty of Portsmouth in 1905, which settled the Russo-Japanese conflict and resulted in a Nobel Peace Prize for his efforts. Teddy also symbolically served notice that the U.S. was a new world power by commissioning the global odyssey of the Great White Fleet. Construction of the Panama Canal also began during the Roosevelt administration. The death of Queen Victoria in 1901 marked the close of an era in Great Britain. Admiral Peary's disputed discovery of the North Pole was the big story as the decade came to a close.

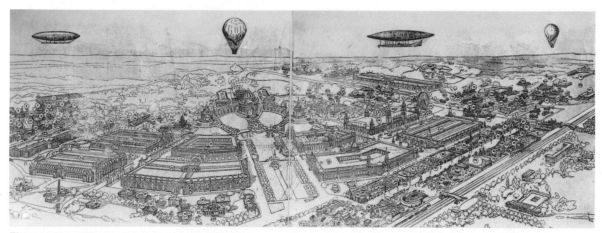

The magnificent World's Fair that celebrated the 100th year of the Louisiana Purchase attracted millions of visitors to St. Louis. The spacious fairgrounds were depicted as above in The St. Louis Post-Dispatch in 1904.

The tragic San Francisco earthquake and fire was a national distraction from baseball's season opening in April of 1906.

The death of Britain's Queen Victoria signaled the beginning of the end of the so-called Victorian Age in 1901.

THE FANS

Although baseball's popularity was nationwide in 1900, the major league arena was exclusive to the northeast quadrant of the U.S., with St. Louis the westernmost city and only Baltimore and Washington barely beneath the Mason-Dixon line. The vast majority of fans who actually attended games were the residents of the large urban areas with major league franchises. The rest of the population focused attention on their own local teams and followed the big leagues in local newspapers and national publications. Thus the average fan (or "bug" or "crank", as they were called), whose ticket purchase supported major league baseball operations, had a distinctly urban profile with a iifestyle that set him apart from the followers of the game who resided in the hinterlands.

America at the turn of the century was experiencing the peak period of European immigration. The vast majority of these immigrants settled in the large cities of the Northeast and took to baseball as an affordable outlet for recreation. Although the game had a genuine following among the intellectuals and the affluent, it was supported at the gate by the working class, a large percentage of which consisted of first and second generation European immigrants. Despite the general prohibition of Sunday baseball, an afternoon at the ballpark was a popular and relatively inexpensive way for the urban work force to occupy their leisure hours. Unlike today's casual fans, the average fan of 1900 would dress up "properly" whenever he or she left home for the afternoon, whether it was for a baseball game or church or a picnic in the nearest park. Full suits complete with derby hats were the rule rather than the exception in the baseball crowds of that decade. In spite of the tarnished reputation that baseball had, there was usually a contingent of escorted ladies in their "Sunday" best in attendance. Sprinkled among the hordes of drably repetitive suited males were the brightly colored chapeaus of the lady fans. During 1907 and 1908, the fashion fad in women's wear was the gigantic "Merry Widow" hat, which often caused a furor with the unlucky fan whose view of the field was severely restricted. Management was pressured to urge the lady fan so dressed to uncover her tresses for the sake of order in the stands. Fortunately, the fashion was short-lived and ladies soon adopted less controversiai headgear for their outings.

The latest fashions as displayed in the 1908 Sears & Roebuck catalogue.

A gentleman fan and his date strolling up the ramp to the grandstand of New York's Polo Grounds around 1908.

The infamous fashion fad of 1907-08, the "Merry Widow" hat—not a welcome sight for serious baseball fans seeking an unobstructed view of the game.

The City of Boston claimed two of the greatest "superfans" of the decade, or possibly of any decade in the history of major league baseball. The "royal rooters," as they were called, were led by one Mike Regan and a colorful character known as Ned "Nuf Sed" McGreevy. McGreevy owned a saloon in the neighborhood of the South End Grounds that was a popular watering-hole for local sports heroes, notables, and neighborhood baseball "cranks." Before the American Leaguers appeared on the Huntington Avenue site, which was just over the tracks from South End, McGreevy was the unofficial leader of dedicated followers who attended the National League games in the 1890's. When the popular Jimmy Collins and other South End favorites jumped to the American League in 1901, McGreevy and his legions followed suit and became a fixture at Huntington Avenue. Pennant-winning teams in 1903-04 contrasted by dismal National League teams only solidified the newfound popularity of American League baseballers in the Hub. McGreevy and his noisy, pennant-waving entourage would monopolize a sizeable section of the main grandstand with vocal support. A popular song of the day, "Tessie," became their battle cry as they hooted and hollered the Boston team to victory over the Pirates in the first World Series in the fall of 1903. McGreevy's crowd even made the excursion to Pittsburgh's Exposition Park to make their presence felt in the games played there. It is not recorded who "minded the store" while "Nuf Sed" conducted his many pilgrimages to Huntington Avenue and even to the deep South during spring training. McGreevy's highly visible presence as the leader of Boston's rooters persisted into the decade of the teens and the remnants of his collection of baseball photos that graced the walls of his legendary saloon are a prized possession of the Boston Public Library.

"Nuf Sed" McGreevy's crowd of "royal rooters" attracted the attention of everyone in attendance at Boston's Huntington Avenue Grounds.

NEWSPAPERS AND PERIODICALS

The daily newspapers, particularly in the major league towns, were the window to the baseball world for the typical fans of the game in the early 1900's. Keeping informed of the daily happenings on the diamond could only be done by devouring the sports pages of a wide choice of dailies offered via home delivery or on the newsstands all over town. With no radio or television to provide instant coverage of the games or, for that matter, all news of the day, the newspaper industry enjoyed its zenith of popularity. Readers had a choice of anywhere from four to twelve papers to choose from in the larger urban centers, and competition was fierce in the dissemination of the latest scores and gossip during the summer months. Many dailies produced "sporting extras" which printed the line scores of local games up to the last inning played at press time. Important games, especially down the pennant stretch and at World Series time, would result in delayed editions that would not hit the presses until the final results could be published. Many of the newspaper's downtown offices would provide graphic bulletin boards where hordes of excited fans could follow the progress of the games from a downtown sidewalk location. Even the more stuffy papers, whose editorial stance tried to minimize the importance of sporting news, could not ignore the obvious circulation bonus that up-to-date baseball coverage would produce.

Reporting baseball was front-page material for competing newspapers, especially during the crucial days of the pennant races.

A sizable crowd of fans milling around a makeshift "scoreboard" at a downtown Cincinnati newspaper office building.

If the daily newspaper was the window to the baseball world, the baseball writers were the eyes and ears of the fans who could not attend all games in person, but were determined to stay informed on a daily basis. Unfortunately for many competent journalists, most major newspapers of the period avoided bylines and the daily reporting of baseball was often anonymous as far as the average reader was concerned. Many skillful writers remained unrecognized during their careers while others, because of the editorial policy of the papers they worked for, gained reputations that did not necessarily reflect their eminence over their peers. However, the baseball writers whose names were familiar to readers were generally masters of their craft and the newspapers they worked for were gradually discovering that publicizing their names meant increased circulation. Charles Dryden was a good example of a "known" baseball writer whose printed byline sold papers. Dryden was a much-traveled newspaper reporter who migrated to the West Coast and back to New York in the nineties. Working for the New York Journal in spring training of 1898, he offended Giants owner Andy Freedman and was subsequently barred from the Polo Grounds for that season. But the determined Dryden managed to cover the baseball season by proxy, using the reports of other writers. The publicity surrounding the incident actually helped his career opportunities, as the Philadelphia North American hired him in 1900 to report baseball, complete with identifying byline and accompanying photo. The restless Mr. Dryden moved to the Chicago American in 1902 and then back to the Philadelphia North American in 1903. The Chicago Tribune lured him back to the Windy City in 1907 and gave him star billing on their sports staff. His popular and amusing style of prose made him one of the charmed circle of baseball writers who were granted columns under their own names. By the end of the decade, many more major newspapers were promoting the "cult" following of favored writers, granting them columnist status and using their names to promote circulation. In spite of the highly competitive and possessive nature of the newspaper business of that era, the writers finally joined forces and formed the Baseball Writers Association in 1908. By bonding together, they continually improved their standing with their employers and with club owners, and elevated their level of recognition among the baseball public.

The other members of the newspaper sporting departments that "came of age" in the decade were the artists and photographers. At the turn of the century, half-toned photographs were rarely used on the sports pages and those that appeared were posed studio-type portraits which could be used repeatedly as "window-dressing." Some of the wealthier or more progressive papers exploited this new technology to their advantage, but many others survived with little or no photography. Line artists and cartoonists provided much of the visual enhancements to the baseball reports. Some newspapers would painstakingly trace over actual photographs to present line art renditions rather than print the actual photograph itself. The styles of line illustrations that graced the sports pages varied widely, from stiff representational sketches to absurdly amusing cartoon styles. The skills of the cartoonists ranged from the crudely amateur to the incredibly gifted. Wallace Goldsmith of the Boston Herald and Globe shared his talents among the various newspaper staffs, but devoted most of his efforts to an almost daily cartoon montage of happenings at the local baseball game of the day. His caricatures of the local favorites and visiting players as well were a popular feature for Boston fans. The whimsical, humoristic cartoon treatment of the game highlights provided relief from the columns of prose one had to wade through to get a full report of the day at the local baseball park. One of the premier line artists, whose cartoon style reflected lighthearted humor without sacrificing his clearly expert artistic skill, was J. Normand Lynd. Lynd's cartoons first appeared in the NY Herald late in the decade and continued well into the next decade.

Cartoonist Wallace Goldsmith entertained Boston baseball readers with almost daily cartoon reports of the home games in the Boston Herald.

The New York Herald displayed the artistic talent of J. Norman Lynd on their sporting pages beginning late in the decade.

Some examples of traced-over photos by newspaper artists. The likenesses were sometimes uncanny in their fidelity to the originals.

Original photographs of game action were carefully traced into line drawings—a much more dependable medium for newspaper reproduction at the turn of the century.

In 1900, few newspapers had their own photographers on the payroll—at least not exclusively devoted to sports departments or baseball in particular. Team photographs and posed portraits provided by studio professionals comprised most of the baseball photography used by newspapers in the early 1900's. The Boston area had the most prolific source of this type of photography, notably the studios of Elmer Chickering and Carl J. Horner. Horner, in particular, deserved special recognition for his diligent photo documentation of player portraits in the 1900-09 period. Besides the individual players of both local Boston teams, nearly every player on all the visiting major league clubs sat for their portrait in Horner's Boston studio during the middle years of the decade. These portraits (in uniform shirts but capless) were printed and published everywhere—in the Spalding/Reach Guides, in Sporting Life, and in composite team montages that still survive in original print form. These detailed studies have furnished a permanent collection of the likenesses of most of the big league players of the period and, in the case of many players, the only surviving photograph. The portraits by Horner are in abundance in the TEAMS section of this volume and we must be grateful that, because of his thorough work, we have a very good idea of what these men looked like.

As the decade rolled on, photographic coverage of baseball gradually introduced more and more posed action and genuine action shots. When the lighting was good, pitchers could actually be photographed in the act of delivery, resulting in much more animated photos to dress up the sporting pages of the newspapers. Photographers and their bulky, often tripod-mounted box cameras could position themselves along the edges of the playing field and capture the players in more action-oriented situations. By the middle of the decade, actual game action photos were being published in the next day's issues. Readers were getting a more candid and revealing look at baseball via the printed page with the advent of increased action photography. Some newspapers even hired their own cameramen to cover baseball and, of course, other events during the off season. As more and more lensmen congregated along the sidelines of the playing field, they became a nuisance and an obstruction to players in pursuit of foul balls or errant throws. In 1910, new NL President Tom Lynch finally banished cameramen from the field of play, a necessary decision that was loudly protested by the newspapers.

Among the notable pioneers in this new form of baseball photography were William Keunzel of the Detroit News and Louis Van Oeyen of the Cleveland Press. Much of their work has survived either in original prints or numerous published versions. The master of the posed action shot was Charles Conlon in New York. Just as Horner had provided a complete, head and shoulders record of the players in his heyday, Conlon managed to document most of the players of later seasons with a marvelous portfolio of expertly composed action poses. Fortunately, many of Conlon's original works have survived and are currently in the custody of The Sporting News in St. Louis.

Groups of camera artists on the field were a common sight at New York's Polo Grounds.

About 1905, Charles Conlon began a long career of documenting the major leaguers of four decades on film. This on-the-field portrait of Christy Mathewson was one of his earliest works.

A typical application of the widely published studio portraits by Boston's Horner.

Cleveland's Louis Van Oeyen was an early master of game action photography. Willie Keeler of NY is shown beating out a throw at League Park in 1906.

For the genuine baseball "cranks" who could not get enough inside dope on the game in the hometown dailies, two very fine and thorough weekly newspapers devoted to baseball were available on a national basis. THE SPORTING NEWS was published in St. Louis (as it is to this day) on a year-round basis and sold for 5 cents on the newsstands. It published full reports by correspondents from all the major league cities and printed box scores and game reports during the season. SPORTING LIFE provided similar reporting, but in tabloid form, on a year-round weekly schedule. Philadelphia was the place of publication, so it followed that its readership was heavily eastern, even though its coverage was geographically as balanced as The Sporting News. For reasons unknown, Sporting Life gave a regular appendix coverage of trap shooting—a curious choice of subject matter to complement its main menu of baseball. Both periodicals were tightly structured and consistent in format, with limited use of photographs.

Although baseball coverage was a regular feature in many popular magazines of the day, such as Frank Leslie's Illustrated Weekly and Police Gazette, not until 1908 did the national game claim a magazine of its own. BASEBALL MAGAZINE began publishing in Boston on a year-round monthly basis with a fine staff of experienced writers and a generous use of first-rate photographs. During the winter months, occasional articles on football and other sporting activities would help fill the void, but baseball was its reason for being. It was a hit with serious baseball followers right from the start and enjoyed a prosperous existence for over four decades. Erudite baseball fans also looked forward to the annual baseball guide books, especially the Spalding Guide and its nearly identical counterpart, the Reach Guide. Spalding was published in the name of the National League and Reach represented the American League, but each guide covered both leagues. These pocket-size guides contained all the statistics and summaries of the past season including photographs, plus minor leagues and collegiate records. The Spalding/Reach guides have survived as priceless tools for researchers of baseball history.

THE SPORTING NEWS, despite its heavy editorial stance on many controversial issues, was a popular and necessary journal for serious baseball fans.

The Reach/Spalding guides were eagerly received by the baseball public every winter. Many "look-alike" guides appeared from time to time, but failed to dislodge these booklets as the most popular guides.

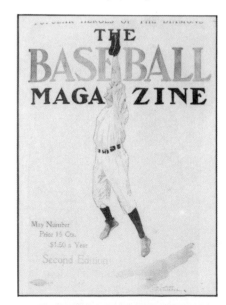

SPORTING LIFE was another weekly tabloid that fed the appetites of baseball cranks all year round.

In 1908, BASEBALL MAGAZINE gave the game a monthly magazine to call its own.

THE BALLPARKS

The baseball parks of 1900-1909 were a far cry from the massive citadels used for today's baseball. Mostly all wooden construction and more intimate in their accommodations, these facilities were truly neighborhood parks. Bordered by normal surface streets and surrounded with whatever type of urban structures the neighborhood provided, whether it happened to be residential, commercial, or industrial, these structures were much more inviting than the totally insulated and isolated architectural monstrosities of today. Since most fans used public transportation to get to the park and automobiles had not yet become a major contributor to traffic congestion, there was no need for expansive parking lots on or near stadium property. Streetcars, subways, and urban trains would strain their capacities with hordes of passengers headed to and from the games. A fully enclosed and shielded baseball park was unheard of in those days, and anywhere a fan sat he could see at least some of the surrounding neighborhood and never lose a sense of where he was. Total seating capacity averaged around 15,000 and overflow crowds were accommodated by allowing fans to stand around the outfield perimeters behind ropes. This arrangement forced the implementation of makeshift ground rules which altered the outcome of many games, but with equal effects that may or may not have favored the home team. Prices ranged from $1 for the main covered grandstand to 25 cents for the remote bleachers.

Hordes of ticket buyers converge on the main entrance of Detroit's Bennett Park for the 1909 World Series. Note the carriages parked along Trumbull Avenue.

The rooftops of the numerous apartment buildings that surrounded Philadelphia's Columbia Avenue Park are filled with fans eager to get a free view of a crucial Athletics vs. Detroit contest in 1907.

Most of the enormous crowd that witnessed the 1906 World Series at the White Sox home grounds were standees.

The Huntington Avenue streetcars lined up to try to accommodate the throng after the Boston Americans defeated Pittsburgh in the 1903 Fall Classic.

Scorecards were sold at the gate for 5 cents or 10 cents. These cards were not the deluxe, bulky magazines of today, but usually folded, two-page programs with plenty of advertisements and minimal baseball information. Players of both teams were listed, but since no numbers appeared on the uniforms, the only way to identify the players was either from familiarity or word-of-mouth from nearby fans. There were numbering systems used on some scoreboards that could be matched up with the scorecard listings. This was useful only in identifying those players in the game, but was of no value in identification of substitutes on the benches. Although it was part of the umpires' duties, some parks also employed a man with a large megaphone who would bark out the starting lineups and announce substitutions during the game. With no PA systems and no uniform numbers, many a fan sat through an entire game without being sure who did what. Only the white uniforms distinguished the home team from the enemy. There was usually a single scoreboard, manually operated with large cards and located somewhere along the outfield fence. Some of these scoreboards kept track of other ML game scores (received via teletype), but many had only the inning-by-inning line score of the game at hand. The games would begin (or were "called," an expression of the day that contradicts present usage) at 2:00 or as late as 4:00 pm, presumably to attract truants or late-comers who might try to take in the game after work.

Most of the architectural details of the post-1900 major league grandstands were of standard board lumber construction, including a wooden roof. The most grandiose of the all-wooden parks was New York's Polo Grounds, a giant horseshoe with the major league's largest full upper deck. Partly due to strict building codes, Boston's two neighboring ballparks were the most unusual in their structure and appearance. The foundations were basically brick and mortar with interconnected low-profile peaked tin roofs. The overall look was somewhat "Moorish," with arched openings and steel girder roof supports. Cincinnati's Palace of the Fans had a unique classical Romanesque decor, but its architectural flair was its own undoing. Its small seating capacity could not be expanded without destroying the architectural integrity and it was eventually razed in 1912 in favor of a modern steel-and-concrete facility. Another unusual architectural feature of the period was the "cantilever" upper grandstand construction of Philadelphia's National League Park (later known as Baker Bowl). Gigantic brick tower structures acted as bridge supports for the spans of the upper deck, minimizing the need for numerous support post obstructions.

A view of the left field corner at Brooklyn's Washington Park. The outfield clubhouse was a typical arrangement in the early 1900's.

Detroit's hard-hitting outfielder Sam Crawford poses in front of the scoreboard and clubhouse in deep centerfield at Bennett Park.

By the turn of the century, all major league parks provided clubhouse facilities with varying degrees of accommodations, including shower baths. But up to 1907, these conveniences were available only to the home team. Visiting clubs were previously required to suit up in their hotel rooms and parade to the grounds in open carriages or trolleys—along city streets often populated with hostile partisans. The clubhouse was usually a separate structure set apart from the grandstands and ticket offices and often located in the far reaches of the outfield. An exception to this was Boston's Huntington Avenue Grounds, which provided clubhouse facilities for both teams under the grandstands. In 1905, the Cubs built a relatively magnificent colonial brick clubhouse in the centerfield of their West Side Grounds, complete with rooftop bleachers.

Dignitaries and the press shared the small cupola on the grandstand roof of the American League park in Baltimore.

The players' bench in Boston typified the turn-of-the-century version of dugouts.

Since the baseball writers were the only media link with the paying customers (the fans), all clubs had the wisdom to provide the press with adequate facilities, including a good vantage point of the game. In some parks, the press had its own exclusive cubicle on the grandstand roof, while others had a press section in the box seat area at field level. The Detroit club hastily fabricated a press box on the first base pavilion roof at Bennett Park for the 1907 World Series, but their good intentions backfired on them. Inadequate shelter from miserable weather conditions and a crude ladder access created a furor with visiting reporters. Boston's Huntington Avenue grandstand structure included comfortable office quarters exclusively for newspapermen.

Dugouts, as we knew them in following decades, did not exist in the old wooden parks of the early 1900's. Players' benches were at field level, usually flush against the front of the grandstand and protected with an overhung roof. The players' benches at Milwaukee's Lloyd St. Grounds in 1901 were the lone throwback to the 19th century. Early photographs show the players seated on open park benches along first and third base and far removed from the stands.

An important source of additional revenue for major league clubs was the rental of advertising space on the fences or wherever a sales message could be highly visible to park patrons. Colorful billboards that promoted products, local merchants, and even political campaigns were in abundance at post-1900 ballparks. Rewards of prize money or merchandise were offered to players who could manage to drive a baseball against or over a particular sign, usually requiring a Herculean effort to do so. The best known promotion of

this type appeared in many of the parks at the close of the decade. The Bull Durham Tobacco company displayed their trademark bull image in a distant corner of the outfield fence and had a standing offer of $50 plus samples of their tobacco to any player who could hit their billboard on the fly. The winners were well publicized in Bull Durham ads nationwide.

In 1900, the many fans who did not use public transport to get to the games and lived too far away to walk would arrive by some form of horse-drawn conveyance. Private carriages, cabs for hire, and tally-hos (a horse-drawn precursor of buses) were in abundance and the ballclubs provided whatever extra space was available for hitching the horses and parking the carriages. Some parks provided roofed carriage sheds to accommodate as many carriages as they could. Others resorted to curbside hitching posts and vacant lots in the surrounding neighborhood, creating a congestion that automobiles would enlarge upon in later decades. The Polo Grounds in those early years would permit the private carriages to be parked in a semi-circle around the centerfield perimeter. By the end of the decade, fewer and fewer horses were in evidence as the newfangled automobiles began to dominate the urban landscape. The game's popularity was increasing in leaps and bounds and steadily rising attendance soon made it clear that the majority of the smaller wooden parks were incapable of handling the growing crowds and the abundance of automobiles. Larger, more fireproof grandstands of concrete and steel began to surface in 1909 and continued to be built in the major league cities in the following years. By 1920, only St. Louis's Robison Field survived as the last reminder of the pre-1910 era of wooden grandstands.

By the end of the decade, the outfield fences at New York's Hilltop Park were covered with billboards. Note the famous Bull Durham sign in centerfield.

A stream of fans filing out of Boston's Huntington Avenue grandstand after a big game. Most were on their way to board trolley cars for their homeward journey.

OPENING DAY CEREMONIES

Opening day ceremonies were a much more ceremonial and festive occasion than in subsequent decades. The grandstands would be generously decorated with patriotic trimmings that are rarely seen now. Even the groundskeepers participated in dressing up the diamond markings with elaborate and sometimes bizarre chalk decorations, which were short-lived after game action took its toll. A popular local band would be engaged to entertain the baseball-hungry audience, who would fill the park long before game time. The band would play a medley of patriotic songs, marches, and popular tunes of the day. Many traditions were observed that were faithfully conducted on all opening days well into the twentieth century. A well-publicized parade through the streets that led to the park would feature local dignitaries, fan support clubs, and the players themselves (in uniform)—all in full view from open carriages (mostly horse-drawn, but automobiles were used more and more later in the decade). In Brooklyn, opening day festivities would not be complete without Shannon's 23rd Regiment Band, a local fixture at Washington Park openers. In Detroit, former catching hero Charley Bennett would be present to receive the ceremonial opening pitch from the mayor or other local dignitary. Bennett had been the star backstop on the 1887 Detroit champions and his local popularity was fortified by the tragic loss of both legs in a freak train-station accident in 1894. Bennett continued this role in Detroit openers until his death in the 1920's.

The highlight of opening day pre-game doings was the flag raising ceremony. In most cases, the flag to be raised was Old Glory, but if the club had won the league championship the year before, a pennant-raising was also in order. Sometimes this opportunity was so sacred that a special date was set aside sometime after opening day for the occasion, but after the world championship became an additional prize that deserved a special day, the less prestigious league pennant-raising was sometimes included in the flag raising performed at the opener. In the earlier years of the decade, winning the pennant in a given year signified the championship of the following season, a source of some confusion in examining the historical artifacts of those years. The players of both teams played an integral part in the flag raising ritual, usually forming an orderly, rank-and-file procession to the flag pole. Team captains or managers did the honors of hoisting the cloth while the band played on. Once that task was completed, they would once again close ranks and return in military fashion across the playing field to congregate at the grandstand or home plate area. There

they would be greeted by local dignitaries, who would offer a brief address. Among the customary blessings to bring the team luck were presentations of loving cups and elaborate floral arrangements with messages of hope for a successful season. The ceremonial first pitch, usually performed by the mayor or the most prominent official in attendance, would close out the festivities and the umpire would order the game to commence. It was grand theater for the vast hordes of fans present, even though most of them were unable to hear what was being said.

Charles Bennett, a great catcher for Detroit in the 1880's, had the local park named after him. His presence at home openers became a tradition.

The Washington and Boston clubs assemble in deep centerfield at Huntington Avenue Grounds for the ceremonial flag raising at the 1906 opener.

Catcher/Manager Billy Sullivan poses with the usual floral blessings that were a standard feature of opening days throughout the majors.

THE TEAMS AND THE PLAYERS

The rules decreed that team rosters were to be 14 to 16 players, but it was not enforced as many teams exceeded the limit if they chose to stretch their salary outlays. Budgets for most club owners provided their own restraints on the number of players they were willing to carry on the payroll. Player/managers were commonplace during the decade—a bargain for tight-fisted owners who were able to squeeze two salaries into one by the process. In the early years of the decade, only one coach was permitted on the field and he could switch back and forth between the first and third base coaching positions, whichever best suited the strategy of the moment. Full-time coaches were non-existent for most of the decade and in most cases the job on the baselines was performed by either the manager himself or a trusted veteran player selected off the bench. Pitchers were very often used for coaching duties since they did not play every day anyway. In 1908, Kid Gleason of the Phillies and Deacon McGuire with Cleveland became the first non-playing coaches on a major league payroll. It was more accidental than intentional, since both veteran players had anticipated limited game appearances when they were hired. Arlie Latham and Duke Farrell adopted similar coaching positions the following season (1909) with the New York teams, but the practice remained a rarity with other clubs for another decade or more.

Many teams retained mascots, sometimes animals but usually young boys who also performed menial clubhouse chores for the players—a precursor of today's batboys. Some mascots were, however, kept around for reasons of superstition more than for their utilitarian value. Or in some cases, the boy happened to be the son of the manager or of a club official. The "Jim Crow" mentality of baseball at that time permitted an occasional negro boy as mascot—probably well treated, but looked upon more as a house pet and good luck charm than as a useful employee.

All clubs had a team captain, designated by the manager—usually a veteran player, and in most cases a star performer. The role was somewhat coveted if for no other reason than it provided a salary bonus of several hundred dollars. The role of the captain was largely ceremonial, but he did assume certain important duties during the course of a game, such as dictating exactly where the fielders should position themselves and calling the umpire's attention to rules violations. The captain served a useful purpose to bench managers by delivering the lineup cards to the umpire and keeping the umpire informed of player substitutions. However, many of the player/managers of the period also included these captain's duties in their managing routine and made the need for a field captain redundant and pointless. Perhaps because of this, the practice of naming a field captain eventually died out in subsequent decades.

As the game became more "civilized" with the new curbs on rowdyism, some of the "ruffian" trappings also fell out of fashion. The last handlebar mustaches were shaved off by Jake Beckley in 1907 and finally John Titus in 1908. Nevertheless, the average professional baseball player at the turn of the century was poorly educated and came from a lower class background. There were exceptions, of course, including a sprinkling of college men and indeed some from the graduate levels. Hugh Jennings, despite his association with the old Baltimore hooligans, had a law degree from Cornell. As many as ten major leaguers had doctorates in medicine or dentistry and, accordingly, every one was nicknamed DOC. Since blacks were excluded, other lower income levels of American society furnished a bumper crop of candidates. The "Shanty" Irish were at the bottom of the social ladder in the late 1800's and baseball provided an opportunity for young Irish lads to escape their lot in life. Player rosters abounded with a disproportionate number of Irish names and baseball seemed a nearly exclusive brotherhood of the sons of Erin. Names like Delahanty, McGraw, Burke, Dillon, Grady, O'Brien, Duffy, etc., were the household words of major league baseball. Curiously, other sizable European ethnics in the immigrant population were poorly represented. Ed Abbatichio was possibly the only established Italian/American in the major leagues at one point—an odd fact in view of the emergence in later decades of numerous stars with Italian surnames.

Detroit's mascot, flanked by Bill Donovan and Germany Schaefer.

TEAM CAPTAINS 1900-1909

National League

BOSTON: Hugh Duffy 1900, Herman Long 1901-02, Fred Tenney 1903-07, Joe Kelley 1908, Mgr. Frank Bowerman 1909

BROOKLYN: Joe Kelley 1900-01, Willie Keeler 1902, Jack Doyle 1903, Frank Dillon 1904, Jimmy Sheckard 1905, Jimmy Casey 1906-07, Harry Lumley 1908-09

CHICAGO: Jimmy Ryan 1900, Jack Doyle 1901, Bobby Lowe 1902-03, Mgr. Frank Chance 1904-09

CINCINNATI: Tom Corcoran 1900-02, Joe Kelley 1903-06, John Ganzel 1907-08, Hans Lobert 1909

NEW YORK: George Davis 1900-01, Jack Doyle 1902, Heinie Smith 1902, Mgr. John McGraw 1903-04, Dan McGann 1905-07, Mike Donlin 1908, Fred Tenney 1909

PHILADELPHIA: Ed Delahanty 1900-01, Roy Thomas 1902-03, Harry Wolverton 1903-04, Kid Gleason 1906-07, Mike Doolan 1908-09

PITTSBURGH: Mgr. Fred Clarke 1900-09

ST. LOUIS: John McGraw 1900, Mgr. Patsy Donovan 1901-03, Jake Beckley 1904, Mgr. Kid Nichols 1905, Dave Brain 1905, Spike Shannon 1906, Shad Barry 1908, Mgr. Roger Bresnahan 1909

American League

BALTIMORE: Mgr. John McGraw 1901, Wilbert Robinson 1901-02, Joe Kelley 1902

NEW YORK: Mgr. Clark Griffith 1903-07, Willie Keeler 1905, '09, Kid Elberfield 1908, Hal Chase 1909

BOSTON: Mgr. Jimmy Collins 1901-06, Chick Stahl 1907, Cy Young 1907, Bob Unglaub 1907-08, Doc Gessler 1909

CHICAGO: Mgr. Clark Griffith 1901-02, Billy Sullivan 1903, Jimmy Callahan 1904, Mgr. Fielder Jones 1905-1908, Mgr. Billy Sullivan 1909

CLEVELAND: Mgr. Jimmy McAleer 1901, Frank Bonner 1902, Nap Lajoie 1902-09

DETROIT: Jimmy Casey 1901-02, Ducky Holmes 1902, Heinie Smith 1903, Charlie Carr 1904, Ed Gremminger 1904, Bobby Lowe 1904, Bill Coughlin 1905-08, Germany Schaefer 1909

MILWAUKEE: Mgr. Hugh Duffy 1901

ST. LOUIS: Dick Padden 1901-05, Bobby Wallace 1906-09

PHILADELPHIA: Nap Lajoie 1901-02, Lave Cross 1902-05, Harry Davis 1905-09

WASHINGTON: Wm. Clarke 1901, Jimmy Ryan 1902, Ed Delahanty 1902-03, Malachi Kittredge 1904, Patsy Donovan 1904, Mgr. Jake Stahl 1905-06, Larry Schlafly 1907, Bob Ganley 1908-09

John Titus, the last major leaguer to sport a mustache.

However, discounting the deliberate exclusion of blacks, the opportunities for a career in baseball were basically open to any young man who demonstrated the necessary skills and competitive nature. Even American Indians, who faced traditional discrimination in other fields, and deaf mutes found their way into the big time. Charles "Chief" Bender, a Chippewa from Minnesota, was a mainstay on Connie Mack's pitching staff for most of the decade. "Dummy" Hoy and "Dummy" Taylor enjoyed successful major league seasons without being distracted by the insensitive nicknames—which they weren't able to hear anyway.

Speaking of nicknames, the 1900-09 period was the heyday of colorful and interesting nicknames. Despite the combative, possessive spirit of the ballplayers of that era (or maybe because of it) hardly a player could pass through the major league scene without being addressed by some epithet that was not his given name. Many such names were overused, especially on rookies, such as "KID" or "BABE," and lost much of their individuality. But an endless litany of unique nicknames became engraved in the folklore of the game. Mordecai Brown was able to overcome the loss of the index finger on his throwing hand and enjoy an illustrious career and an identity as "Three Finger" Brown. Joe McGinnity was forever identified as "Iron Man" from his reputation for pitching both ends of doubleheaders on more than one occasion. Irvin Wilhelm was called "Kaiser" for obvious reasons. No other decade in baseball history could match the collection of unusual nicknames that existed in the 1900-09 period: "Pink" Hawley, "Cozy" Dolan, "Klondike" Douglas, "Brickyard" Kennedy, "Boileryard" Clarke, "Piano Legs" Hickman, "Bones" Ely, "Snake" Wiltse, "Germany" Schaefer, "Rubberlegs" Miller, and "Noodles" Hahn, were among the well-known baseball names of the era. Some nicknames were almost automatic for certain types: Indians were called "Chief," Germans were called "Heinie" or "Fritz," redheads were "Red," and country bumpkin types were "Rube." Effeminate nicknames like "Tillie" and "Kitty" were claimed by players whose masculinity was never in question in the rough and tough world of baseball. The most common nicknames, outside the usual Billies, Jimmies, etc., were DOC, KID, RUBE, RED, and DEACON. Today's "Oil Can" Boyd would be just another nicknamed journeyman in the early 1900's.

The decade also had its share of eccentric and colorful characters among the ranks of major leaguers. George "Rube" Waddell was perhaps the most newsworthy and certainly the most talented of a handful of oddball personalities. Waddell was an overpowering strikeout artist who pitched his way into baseball's Hall of Fame with four different clubs after the turn of the century. In his journey through the decade, he left a legacy of indefensible absenteeism, strange preoccupations with the trivial, and, worst of all, periodic bouts with the bottle. Connie Mack was able to get the most mileage out of the gifted hurler but finally gave up on him and sold him in 1908 to the St. Louis Browns, where he finished his career. Marital problems, alcohol, and pneumonia finally caught up with him and he died at age 38 in 1914. Herman "Germany" Schaefer was the reigning comedian of the period. Schaefer had his best years as a second baseman for Detroit's pennant-winners of 1907-09. A fine heads-up fielder but a weak hitter, Germany never failed to arouse the fans with an endless repertoire of antics. He would turn the pre-game workouts into a sideshow, performing juggling acts and tricks, all the while "mugging" gleefully for the cameramen. On the basepaths, he immortalized the unthinkable stunt of deliberately stealing first while safely on second, his theory being that the move totally confused the enemy and allowed the lead runner to race toward home plate unmolested. The crowd roared with delight when Schaefer would assume coaching duties, for his endless antics upstaged even the highly animated manager Hugh Jennings. Nick Altrock spent most of the decade with the White Sox, winning 20 games for the Comiskeys in 1904-05-06. He was also a gifted clown who honed his act as the decade wore on and his arm wore out. By the next decade he joined forces with Al Schacht in Washington and formed a legendary baseball comedy duet. Arthur "Bugs" Raymond, major league baseball's resident drunk, had a brief pitching career, topped by an 18-12 record for McGraw's Giants in 1909. But his delinquent and errant behavior, caused by his heavy addiction to alcohol, shortened his career and in due time cost him his life. Bugs wound up his Giant pitching days in 1911, and died from his habit the following year at age 30.

The colorful eccentric, Rube Waddell, takes his St. Louis teammates for a ride in his new gas buggy in 1908.

A Cleveland newspaper depicted the antics of the popular Germany Schaefer.

Charles Hickman was the Bobo Newson of the early 1900s—he played for no less than seven major league teams during the decade.

In terms of consistent performance throughout the full decade of 1900-1909, four players have to be ranked as the greatest of the period. Other equally great diamond stars had outstanding seasons within the ten-year period, but played only part of the decade or experienced several mediocre seasons within the span (i.e., Delahanty, Burkett, Keeler, Cobb, Speaker, Johnson, and Collins). In the National League, the top pitcher of the decade had to be Christy Mathewson. Matty joined the Giants direct from the Bucknell Campus in 1900 and averaged 27 wins per season from 1901 to 1909, including two no-hitters. Honus Wagner transferred from the defunct Louisville club to join the Pittsburgh Pirates in 1900. For the next ten seasons, his batting averages ranged from a low of .329 to a high of .381 and he led all NL batsmen in seven of those years. He also led in stolen bases five times, along with top figures in other offensive categories during the decade. In the American League, top pitching honors had to go to veteran Cy Young, who started the decade with the NL Cardinals (winning 20 there) and jumped over to the Boston Americans, where he averaged 23 wins per season through 1908. He finished the last year of the decade in Cleveland, winning 19 more victories on the way to his record lifetime total of 511. Old Cy led the Bostons to pennants in 1903 and 1904 and tossed a perfect game in 1904. Napoleon Lajoie was clearly the American League's premier position player of the decade. He began the century with the Philadelphia National Leaguers, hitting .346 in 1900. But Connie Mack persuaded him to join the new Athletics, and he promptly ran away with the batting championship with an astounding .422, still a league record. Troubles in the courts disrupted his 1902 season and he was ultimately transferred to Cleveland, where he compiled a .369 average. The next two years, he reclaimed the batting title with .355 and .381 marks and averaged well over .300 for the balance of the decade. Like Wagner, Nap was also no slouch in the field.

CHRISTY MATHEWSON

HONUS WAGNER

CY YOUNG

NAPOLEON LAJOIE

MAJOR LEAGUE ALL STARS OF THE DECADE • 1900-1909

NATIONAL LEAGUE

Outfielders:

Johnny Bates	Dick Cooley	Harry Lumley	Red Murray	Jimmy Sheckard
Ginger Beaumont	Cozy Dolan	Sherry Magee	Jimmy Ryan	Jimmy Slagle
George Browne	Mike Donlin	Billy Maloney	Frank Schulte	Homer Smoot
Jess Burkett	Patsy Donovan	Sandow Mertes	Cy Seymour	Roy Thomas
Fred Clarke	Davey Jones	Mike Mitchell	Spike Shannon	John Titus

Third Basemen:

Bobby Byrne
Doc Casey
Art Devlin
Eddie Grant
Ed Greminger
Tommy Leach
Mike Mowrey
Harry Steinfeldt
Sammy Strang
Harry Wolverton

Shortstops:

Al Bridwell
Tom Corcoran
Monte Cross
Bill Dahlen
Mike Doolan
Phil Lewis
Joe Tinker
Honus Wagner
Bobby Wallace

Second Basemen:

Larry Doyle
Johnny Evers
John Farrell
Billy Gilbert
Kid Gleason
Miller Huggins
Otto Knabe
Nap Lajoie
Claude Ritchey

First Basemen:

Jake Beckley
Kitty Bransfield
Frank Chance
Jack Doyle
John Ganzel
Tim Jordan
Ed Konetchy
Dan McGann
Fred Tenney

Pitchers:

Red Ames	Kid Nichols
Mordecai Brown	Orval Overall
Howie Camnitz	Jack Pfiester
Bill Duggleby	Deacon Phillipe
Bob Ewing	Togie Pittinger
Noodles Hahn	Ed Reulbach
Jack Harper	Tully Sparks
Frank Kitson	Jess Tannehill
Sam Leever	Dummy Taylor
Lefty Leifield	Jack Taylor
Carl Lundgren	Jake Weimer
Nick Maddox	Vic Willis
Christy Matthewson	Hooks Wiltse
Joe McGinnity	

Catchers:

Bill Bergen	Johnny Kling
Brank Bowerman	Larry McLean
Roger Bresnahan	Wilbert Robinson
Red Dooin	Jack Warner
George Gibson	

Utility Players:

Ed Abbaticchio (2B, SS)
John "Shad" Barry (infield, outfield)
Dave Brain (infield, outfield)
Ed Delahanty (1B, outfield)
Jack Dunn (pitcher, infield, outfield)
Solly Hoffman (infield, outfield)
John Hummel (infield, outfield)
Joe Kelley (1B, outfield)
Hans Lobert (SS, 3B)

AMERICAN LEAGUE

Outfielders:

Jimmy Barrett	Sam Crawford	Topsy Hartsell	Willie Keeler	Tris Speaker
Harry Bay	Patsy Dougherty	Charles Hemphill	Matty McIntyre	Chick Stahl
Joe Birmingham	Elmer Flick	Bill Hinchman	Clyde Milan	George Stone
Jess Burkett	Doc Gessler	Danny Hoffman	Ollie Pickering	
Ty Cobb	Danny Green	Davey Jones	Kip Selbach	
	Ed Hahn	Fielder Jones	Socks Seybold	

Third Basemen:

Frank Baker
Bill Bradley
Doc Casey
Jimmy Collins
Bill Coughlin
Lave Cross
Harry Lord
George Moriarty

Shortstops:

Jack Barry
Joe Cassidy
Monte Cross
George Davis
Kid Elberfield
George McBride
Charley O'Leary
Fred Parent
Terry Turner
Heinie Wagner
Bobby Wallace

Second Basemen:

Eddie Collins
Jim Delahanty
Hobe Ferris
Nap Lajoie
Danny Murphy
Dick Padden
Germany Schaefer
Jimmy Williams

First Basemen:

John Anderson
Hal Chase
Harry Davis
Jiggs Donahue
Tom Jones
Candy Lachance
Claude Rossman
Jake Stahl
George Stovall

Pitchers:

Nick Altrock	Al Orth
Chief Bender	Frank Owen
Jack Chesbro	Barney Pelty
Bill Dinneen	Eddie Plank
Frank Donahue	Jack Powell
Bill Donovan	Frank Smith
Clark Griffith	Willie Sudhoff
Harry Howell	Ed Summers
Long Tom Hughes	Jess Tannehill
Walter Johnson	Rube Waddell
Addie Joss	Ed Walsh
Ed Killian	Doc White
Earl Moore	Cy Young
George Mullin	

Catchers:

Harry Bemis	Boss Schmidt
Nig Clarke	Ossie Schreckengost
Lou Criger	Gabby Street
Jim McGuire	Billy Sullivan
Wilbert Robinson	

Utility Players:

Jimmy Callahan (pitcher, outfield)
Ed Delahanty (1B, outfield)
Buck Freeman (1B, outfield)
Charles Hickman (pitcher, infield, outfield)
Frank Isbell (all positions)
Lee Tannehill (SS, 3B)

THE MANAGERS

Since no club consistently dominated its league throughout the decade, it would be difficult to single out the best manager of the period—that is, if winning championships is the principal criterion for such a tribute. In fact, only three managers survived the entire decade: Fred Clarke, Connie Mack, and James McAleer. Each club had its ups and downs, indeed for some it was pretty much down for all ten seasons. The Boston Nationals, except for a third-place finish under A.C. Buckenberger in 1902, finished at or well under .500 all through the decade. Bill Shettsline kept his Philadelphia Nationals in contention the first two seasons of the decade, but it was basically middle of the pack finishes after that for the Phillies. It was the same scenario in Brooklyn. After a pennant in 1900 and third place the following year, the Brooklyns gradually disappeared into the second division for the remainder of the ten-year period. Ned Hanlon, one of the more knowledgeable baseball strategists of his time, lost 104 games in 1905 and bowed out as Brooklyn Manager to try his luck in Cincinnati. Popular player/manager Joe Kelley had been unable to lead the Reds into serious contention and his successor, Hanlon, fared no better. The St. Louis Cardinals, under a parade of managerial changes, went through the entire decade as an also-ran. Cardinal managers' problems were compounded by the constant meddling of owner Frank Robison, the George Steinbrenner of his era. These losing clubs were wounded badly by the American League raids and were never able to rebuild and recover.

Certainly the most successful managers in the National League were Pittsburgh's Fred Clarke and Chicago's Frank Chance—both player/managers. Clarke's Pirate teams won championships at the beginning and the end of the decade and Chance's Cubs were the elite of 1906-08. John McGraw's credentials as a scrappy, tyrannical molder of winning teams also deserves recognition despite his unsavory reputation for unsportsmanlike behavior. A managerial flop in Baltimore, McGraw jumped back to his old league with the New York Giants in mid-1902, and within three years delivered two pennants and a world championship in 1905. Only the controversial Merkle "boner" deprived him of stealing another flag away from the mighty Cubs in 1908. McGraw's claim as a truly great manager would be more firmly established in the following decades.

NED HANLON
Brooklyn
Cincinnati

FRED CLARKE
Pittsburgh

CONNIE MACK
Philadelphia AL

CLARK GRIFFITH
Chicago AL
New York AL

JIMMY McALEER
Cleveland
St. Louis AL

Jimmy McAleer's long tenure with the American League St. Louis Browns began well, finishing second in 1902. But the hapless Brownies, despite the windfall of premium deserters from the cross-town Cardinals, quickly disappeared into second division oblivion for the rest of his managerial career—except for a fourth-place finish in 1908. The Washington Senators, led by a revolving door of impotent managers—Manning, Loftus, Donovan, Stahl, and Cantillon—set the decade standard for ineptitude. They never once surfaced from the second division and finished dead last four times. Clark Griffith pitched and managed Comiskey's White Stockings to the AL pennant in 1901, the league's first big league season. Connie Mack (né Cornelius McGillicuddy) took the AL honors the next year with his Philadelphia Athletics and kept his team in contention the rest of the decade. Mack, incidentally, never donned an Athletics uniform and became conspicuous in later decades because of it. However, many of the other ML field managers in the post-1900 decade also preferred to remain in street clothes, so Connie was not unique in his early years as the A's field boss. Another popular player/manager, Jimmy Collins, led his Boston Americans to successive flags in 1903 and 1904 and enjoyed the glory of managing the first winner of the modern World Series in 1903. Collins was denied the opportunity to repeat in 1904 when the NL champion Giants refused to participate in the post-season series. Connie Mack recaptured the AL bunting in 1905, but lost the world championship to McGraw's Giants. Clark Griffith was lured away from

Chicago to manage the newly formed American League New York club in 1903 and nearly stole the AL flag the following season, losing on the final day on a fateful wild pitch by his 41-game winner, Jack Chesbro. Meanwhile, in Chicago, pitcher Jimmy Callahan replaced Griffith as field boss, then yielded the position to outfielder Fielder A. Jones, who led the White Stockings to a strong third-place finish in 1904. Jones' club narrowly missed winning it all in 1905, but the so-called "hitless wonders" edged out Griffith's New Yorkers for the 1906 pennant and then became the stuff of legends as they outpitched and outhit the powerful cross-town Cubs in the world's championship series, the only all-Chicago Fall Classic to date. The White Sox remained a contender in following seasons, but Jones wearied of the job and relinquished it to catcher Billy Sullivan in 1909. Cleveland's superstar second baseman, Nap Lajoie, joined the ranks of player/-managers in 1905 and finished out the decade as field boss of the "Naps," as they were named in his honor. Lajoie kept the Naps in contention as manager—indeed he narrowly missed the flag in 1908—but the stress of managing took its toll on the Frenchman. Although still among the leaders, his player stats slipped and he eventually resigned to devote his attention to full-time playing. Once relieved of managerial chores, his batting average soared back to earlier levels and we can speculate that his career statistics might have been even more phenomenal without the burden of manager's duties.

JIMMY COLLINS
Boston AL

FRANK CHANCE
Chicago NL

JOHN McGRAW
Baltimore AL
New York NL

FIELDER JONES
Chicago AL

HUGH JENNINGS
Detroit

Certainly the most celebrated American League manager of the closing years of the decade was Detroit's Hugh Jennings. Jennings was hired to replace the stoic Bill Armour in 1907 and promptly lit a fire under the Tiger team. A product of the aggressive school of the old Baltimore Orioles, Jennings introduced a fiery, reckless style of attack that gave the Detroit club consecutive pennants in 1907-08-09. The emergence of young Ty Cobb as a swift, daring baserunner and fearsome batsman was a major factor, but it was the leadership of Jennings that was the catalyst of the team's successes. Jennings' inventive antics on the coaching lines, replete with his famous "ee-yah" battle cry, became the talk of baseball. Unfortunately, the Tiger club was unable to carry the momentum into a post-season championship. losing out in all three seasons and totally embarrassed by the Chicago Cubs in their first two appearances.

THE UMPIRES

Big league umpiring in the post-1900 decade required a stubborn constitution and a thick hide to survive. This was especially true in the older league, where complaints were vehement and physical threats often resulted in bodily injury—not just from angry team members, but the home crowd as well. The league had pathetically weak leadership at the top, and the collective anarchy of independent club owners was unable or unwilling to enforce discipline and ensure protection as did the American League's autocratic Ban Johnson. For much of the decade, only one umpire was used, and the job of calling balls and strikes while trying to make judgement calls all over the playing field made accurate calls throughout the contest difficult at best. Players and managers looked for every opportunity to take advantage of a single umpire's limitations. Unsportsmanlike, outright cheating had become an accepted way to win ball games. Umpires often made critical calls on plays they could not oversee, and both players and fans would react wildly to an unfavorable decision.

To his credit, Ban Johnson did not hesitate to inflict fines or suspensions on players and managers who stepped out of line, and he saw to it that the policies of each team were aimed at preserving law and order. Shortstop Frank Shugart of Chicago felt the fury of Johnson's authority in 1901 when he was banned for life for striking an umpire. The fans appreciated the tighter controls in the new league—one of the reasons why attendance was often surprisingly higher than in the National League. While in Baltimore, John McGraw was among the most villainous umpire-baiters, and his constant run-ins with arbiters was the main reason he feuded with Ban Johnson and abruptly jumped back to the National League. When the National League finally got its house in order, it also saw the wisdom of reinforcing the umpire's authority. By the end of the decade, two umpires were the standard, and rowdy behavior was noticeably less. Even addressing an umpire by anything other than Mr. (last name) was grounds for ejection or fine.

An early 1900's umpire makes the call on a play at home plate. Note chest protector.

RULES, PLAYING CONDITIONS, AND RECORDS

Playing rules, considering the long history of the game, were not all that different from the present, in spite of evolutionary improvements and a vastly changed urban environment. The familiar five-sided home plate design of today was introduced in 1900 to replace a rubberized square that imitated the infield bases. The most significant rule change of the decade was the foul strike rule, implemented by the National League in 1901 to speed up the game. Prior to this rule, foul balls were "neutral" and did not affect the count on the batter. A batter could prolong his turn at bat ad infinitum by fouling off pitch after pitch until he got the one he wanted. This was tiring on the pitcher and did nothing to cultivate interest in the game situation. However, traditionalists in many quarters insisted that the new rule was unjust and consistently called for its revocation for years afterward. But the American League soon adopted the foul strike rule and it became permanent. Other less controversial measures also went into effect in 1901 to improve the game. Catchers were required to position themselves within 10 feet of home plate (which most did anyway by this time), and pitchers were required to deliver the ball as soon as the batter was in the batter's box. The infield dimensions were the same as today during the 1900-09 period: 90 feet between the bases and 60-1/2 feet from the pitching rubber to home plate. The pitching box was elevated, forming a mound as it is at present. The balk rule, always a difficult call, was redefined in 1904. The sacrifice fly rule was introduced in 1908.

Size and specifications of bats and balls were basically the same as today, although the inner component windings of the ball have varied from decade to decade. A variety of methods to doctor up the baseball to the pitcher's advantage were commonplace and perfectly legal. Spit-balls, emery-balls, and other methods of defacing the sphere were tools of the pitching trade. The ball in play not only was kept in play as long as possible, but was soon badly discolored and scuffed as the game progressed. The immaculate white ball of today was a rarity then during a major league contest. Balls that left the playing field were often retrieved and returned to see more game action—a practice that would startle the modern fan. In 1908, a "dull gloss" leather surface was introduced and players were forbidden to rub the new sphere in the dirt or grass, as had been common procedure up to that time.

The custom of using distinctly different sets of uniforms for home and road games was already an established tradition by 1900 and was officially written into the rule book in 1903. The main requirement was

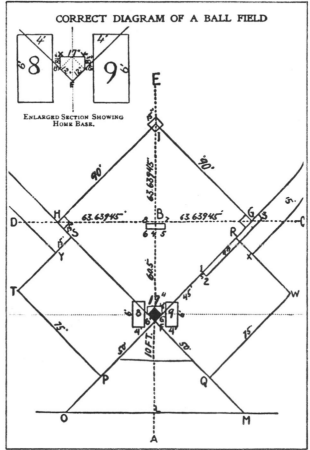

CORRECT DIAGRAM OF A BALL FIELD

ENLARGED SECTION SHOWING HOME BASE.

The layout of a regulation diamond as published in the 1903 Spalding Guide.

A standard base bag and Spalding baseball, the official ball of the National League.

for the home club to wear basically white material for their shirts and trousers, while the visiting club was to wear a gray or other darker fabric. For most teams, a gray duplication of the home whites was the standard for travel, but some opted for a navy blue or other dark shade. With no number identification on the uniforms and no public address system, this uniform feature carried more importance to the average fan then than in more recent decades. From a distance, it was the only positive way to separate the enemy players from the home town heroes. The Chicago Cubs were rebuked by the National Commission after the opening game of the 1907 World Series, when they appeared on their home grounds wearing a specially-made-for-the-occasion gray uniform which was too similar in appearance to the uniforms of the visiting Detroit Tigers. For the following games at the Cubs' West Side Grounds, they were instructed to use the regulation whites that they had worn during the regular season.

Playing fields were not the immaculately manicured lawns of today's natural grass fields. The dirt infields were more likely to contain treacherous pits and valleys that made ground balls do strange things, not to mention the dangerous footing for spikes. However, the conditions varied from park to park and some photographs and written reports of the day suggest that many of the playing surfaces were indeed in top-notch condition. If the fields were as roughly groomed as many historians have determined, the fielding averages would have been significantly lower than they actually were. The ravages of Mother Nature had more effect on playing conditions then. Infields were not covered as they are now, although some teams had begun to experiment with makeshift tarpaulins by the end of the decade. Automatic sprinkler systems and drainage systems in today's outfields were unheard of in the early 1900's. A pre-game deluge would leave the field in an unplayable state and many groundskeeping crews were called upon to perform miracles, given the limited crews and crude equipment available to them. Sawdust was the most common remedy for a muddy field. The parks in Cincinnati and Pittsburgh were occasionally flooded by the adjacent river during heavy spring rains, causing havoc with the schedule. Most outdoor diamonds nowadays are positioned to punish only the right fielder with the glare of afternoon sun. The sun factor was apparently not considered in turn-of-the-century baseball field layouts. The position of the afternoon sun varied from park to park. A left-handed batter in Detroit's Bennett Park had the bright sun of late afternoon directly in his eyes. One wonders if it had any effect on the great Ty Cobb, considering his phenomenal hitting success in the years he played there (1905-1911).

Baseball is a game whose history is interwoven with statistics. Both players and teams were judged by their numbers as much then as they are today. Batting averages, stolen bases, earned run averages, and strikeouts were published and quoted ad infinitum. Box scores were a standard ingredient in the newspaper accounts of the games of the day and their format was basically consistent with today's versions, with minor differences. Some more elaborate box scores included pitcher's records, but in a different format than in modern box scores. But, except for the absence of certain more recent stats, such as RBI's and saves, statisticians and researchers can be very comfortable in extracting important information from these early box scores. The column "H" for hits was more likely labeled 1B or B, which tabulated all hits, not singles only—thus, the same as today's "H" totals. For inexplicable reasons, line scores early in the decade often displayed the home team on the top line rather than on the bottom, as is the standard format today. At season's end, all statistics were carefully reviewed and consolidated into the official body of league statistics. The monstrous task of carefully verifying and compiling these figures was all done by hand arithmetic—no calculators or computers. The results would often alter the final figures from the accumulated periodic totals published during the course of the season. The final official totals would be released late in the year and published widely—in the Spalding/Reach Guides and elsewhere. Considering the vulnerability to serious human errors in compilation and typesetting, the accuracy seems remarkably dependable and immune from suspicion.

BALTIMORE.						ATHLETICS.					
	R.	H.	O.	A.	E.		R.	H.	O.	A.	E.
Gilbert, ss...	1	0	4	5	2	Hartzel, lf..	1	1	0	0	0
Sheckard, cf	1	1	1	0	0	Fultz, 2b....	0	1	2	3	0
Kelley, 3b...	1	1	2	1	0	Davis, 1b....	0	0	11	0	0
Seymour, rf.	1	2	0	0	0	L. Cross, 3b..	0	0	1	3	0
Williams, 2b	1	1	3	5	0	Flick, rf......	1	1	1	0	0
Selbach, lf..	1	2	3	0	0	Seybold, cf..	0	1	1	0	0
McGann, 1b.	0	0	11	0	0	M. Cross, ss.	0	0	2	5	1
Robinson, c.	0	2	3	1	0	Powers, c....	0	2	6	3	0
Hughes, p...	0	0	0	3	0	Plank, p....	0	0	2	2	1
Totals	6	9	27	15	2	Totals	2	6	24	16	2

Score by Innings.

Baltimore	6	0	0	0	0	0	0	x	—6
Athletics	0	1	0	0	0	0	1	0	—2

Two-base hits—Sheckard, Selbach, Robinson (2). Three-base hit—Williams. Sacrifice hits—Seymour, McGann, Fultz, Hughes. Bases stolen—By Hartzel. Double plays—McGann (unassisted), Plank, Powers and Davis; Gilbert, Williams and McGann. Bases on balls—By Hughes, 2; by Plank, 1. Batters hit—By Plank, 2. Struck out—By Plank, 2; by Plank, 4. Left on bases—Baltimore, 5; Athletics, 5. First base on errors—Athletics, 2; Baltimore, 2. Time of game—1:50. Umpire—O'Loughlin. Attendance—2,435.

A 1902 box score. Note that the home team is the TOP line in the SCORE BY INNINGS account.

EQUIPMENT

The tools of the major league baseball trade in the post-1900 decade are looked upon today as primitive, as indeed they were by comparison to the modern arsenal. But at the same time, considering the astounding technological changes over the last 80 years, the paraphernalia of baseball has remained basically unchanged in many aspects. Uniforms were a heavy grade of flannel with a looser, baggier appearance. Laundering was not on a daily basis, especially on the road, and rarely were the flannels enhanced by the luxury of ironing. However, the overall scheme of the baseball player's costume is quite consistent with today. The knicker-style trousers with full stockings, the short-sleeved shirt, and the cap with a sun visor are basic to both present and past. Shirt collars through most of the decade were the full fold-down style, and the popular fad toward the end of the decade was to turn the collar up and affix a safety pin in the front. Laced shirt fronts eventually gave way to buttons by 1910. Belts were noticeably wider in 1900 and more elaborate in construction. Until late in the decade, stockings were one-piece knee-length wool. Then the stirrup style with sanitary undersock was introduced and was soon adopted as standard. Baseball shoes were higher around the ankle, often with replaceable metal spikes. Cap crowns were available in a variety of styles, from a close-fitting rounded shape to the cylindrical, "cheese box" style popularized by the early Shibe Park–era Athletics. Sun visors were shorter than today and some players gave sunglasses a tryout. Catchers' masks were well-made, welded steel wire cages with a leather padded frame. Chest protectors offered about the same protection as today's pneumatic types, but were generally larger and longer. Before Roger Bresnahan opened the 1907 season with his "cricket-style" protective shin guards, catchers' lower legs were vulnerable to painful foul tips or bouncing fast balls. The shin guards were slow to catch on and many catchers stubbornly refused to adopt such an "unmanly" device. Catchers' mitts were large, circular "mattresses." First basemen's mitts were fingerless, rounded mittens, while fielders' gloves were an enlarged mutant of ordinary leather gloves, with a horseshoe of extra padding. Umpires wore the traditional navy blue suit, including a cap style similar to players' caps except that the visor was more abbreviated. Chest protectors and masks for umpires were already standard equipment at the beginning of the decade.

STANDARD BASEBALL EQUIPMENT OF 1900-1909

Spalding's Cotton Web Belts

TRAVEL AND ACCOMMODATIONS

The railroad passenger train system in America at the turn of the century was the principal means of long distance travel and baseball teams spent a good deal of their time on trains. The cost of traveling was always a financial burden and a logistical headache for club owners. Minimizing the amount of train travel was always the primary concern when the leagues plotted out their playing schedules for the approaching season. Road trips were formulated to "hop-scotch" from city to city in as direct a route as possible to cut time and costs. This remains the biggest single reason why major league baseball remained essentially "quarantined" to the northeast corner of the nation (where most of the large cities were anyway) for the first half of the 20th century. Expansion to the West and the South only became possible when air travel could replace train travel. All clubs retained traveling secretaries, who would be responsible for scheduling train trips and coordinating the simultaneous shipment of trunks of equipment and uniforms. Occasionally, these plans would go somehow awry and a visiting team would miss an outgoing train and/or arrive late at their destination. Or, possibly worse yet, the trunks of equipment would be lost. Baseball writers often accompanied the teams and much of their story material would be obtained via hours on end spent socializing with team members in some parlor car. Team members necessarily spent more hours together, which was a mixed blessing. Closer camaraderie and tighter cliques were nurtured, but so were animosities and destructive "hazing" among not-so-compatible teammates. Hotel accommodations were generally in better class establishments and meals were paid for by the club. Hotel lobbies became a gathering place where players would while away the hours in an unfamiliar city. Much mischief and many practical jokes were generated during the long hours spent on trains and in hotels. And, inevitably, frequent arguments and an occasional fistfight would result from the prolonged confinement.

A typical railway parlor car where traveling ballplayers whiled away the hours on the way to the next town.

The Brooklyn club aboard a horse-drawn tally-ho outside their hotel c. 1910.

The Cleveland ballclub boarding their coach en route to an exhibition game in Toledo about 1907.

Some members of the Cleveland Naps pose for a group picture alongside their stopped train.

The Washington team in uniform at a train station somewhere in the South.

SPRING TRAINING

Major league teams at the turn of the century conducted spring training to get players into top physical condition and to look over the newcomers to assess their talents. The goals of the pre-season training ritual were much the same as today, but not nearly as well planned or fully orchestrated as a league-wide exercise. The lengthy interleague exhibition game schedules of today did not exist then. Each club was on its own, making do with whatever arrangement they could manage to afford from year to year. Rather than concentrating on the Florida peninsula, most big league training camps were held in places like Texas, Arkansas, Mississippi, Alabama, Georgia, Northern Florida, and the Carolinas. The Chicago Nationals ventured to far-off California for training from 1903 to 1905. McGraw's Giants and Comiskey's Sox also trekked to the Golden State for training in 1907 and 1908. In 1907 the White Sox broke with the pattern and trained in Mexico City. Any southern resort town with hotel accommodations and a baseball field was a likely candidate, and long-term agreements between a specific club and a specific location were rare. It was an expensive ordeal for the club owners and they often settled for substandard facilities and sometimes hostile communities in order to cut costs. Some training sites were shared with another major league team or a minor league team, and exhibition games with the sharing teams provided an opportunity to obtain revenue from the local fans. Training camps would close up shop weeks before the season opener to allow the teams to "barnstorm" on their long journey northward to help cover the costs of the training sessions. Clubs in some of the major league cities with both American and National League teams would arrive in the home city earliest in order to present a pre-season city series for the local fans. Some teams would pair up and travel north together, playing each other at various whistle stops in order to earn back some of their expenses. If the weather cooperated, the scheme worked well, as the opportunity to see the great star players in person was a rare treat for the fans in smaller cities. The training camps and the northbound odysseys were well covered in the hometown newspapers by the baseball writers who accompanied the team.

The New York Highlanders cavort about their Georgia training grounds via horse-drawn carriage.

Comiskey's Chicago White Sox posing with a new-fangled horseless carriage at their training site in Mexico in 1907.

Some Boston Americans take time off for a hunting trip during spring training at Jacksonville in 1903.

New York's Highlanders working out at Macon, Georgia in 1909.

SPRING TRAINING SITES 1900-1909

National League

BOSTON–1900: Greensboro, NC; 1901: Norfolk, VA; 1902-04: Thomasville, GA; 1905: Charleston, SC; 1906: Jacksonville, FL; 1907: West Baden, IN; 1908-09: Augusta, GA

BROOKLYN–1900: Augusta, GA; 1901: Charlotte, NC; 1902-06: Columbia, SC; 1907-09: Jacksonville, FL

CHICAGO–1900: Selma, AL; 1901-02: Champaign, IL; 1903-05: Los Angeles, CA; 1906-07: Champaign, IL; 1908: West Baden, IN; 1909: Hot Springs, AR

CINCINNATI–1900: New Orleans, LA; 1901-02: (no trip); 1903: Augusta, GA; 1904: Dallas, TX; 1905: Jacksonville, FL; 1906-07: Marlin Springs, TX; 1908: St. Augustine, FL; 1909: Atlanta, GA

NEW YORK–1900-02: (no trip); 1903-05: Savannah, GA; 1906: Memphis, TN; 1907: Los Angeles, CA; 1908-09: Marlin Springs, TX

PHILADELPHIA–1900: Charlotte, NC; 1901: (no trip); 1902: (?); 1903: Richmond, VA; 1904-08: Savannah, GA; 1909: Southern Pines, NC

PITTSBURGH–1900: Thomasville, GA; 1901-09: Hot Springs, AR

ST. LOUIS–1900-02: (no trip); 1903: Dallas, TX; 1904-08: Houston, TX; 1909: Little Rock, AR

American League

BALTIMORE–1901: Hot Springs, AR; 1902: Savannah, GA

NEW YORK–1903-04: Atlanta, GA; 1905: Montgomery, AL; 1906: Birmingham, AL; 1907-08: Atlanta, GA; 1909: Macon, GA

BOSTON–1901: Charlottesville, VA; 1902: Augusta, GA; 1903-06: Macon, GA; 1907-08: Little Rock, AR; 1909: Hot Springs, AR

CHICAGO–1901-02: Excelsior Springs, MO; 1903: Mobile, AL; 1904: Marlin Springs, TX; 1905-06: New Orleans, LA; 1907: Mexico City; 1908: Los Angeles, CA; 1909: San Francisco, CA

CLEVELAND–1901: (no trip); 1902-03: New Orleans, LA; 1904: San Antonio, TX; 1905: New Orleans, LA; 1906: Atlanta, GA; 1907-08: Macon, GA; 1909: Mobile, AL

DETROIT–1901-02: Ypsilanti, MI; 1903-04: Shreveport, LA; 1905-07: Augusta, GA; 1908: Hot Springs, Little Rock, AR; 1909: San Antonio, TX

MILWAUKEE–1901: St. Louis, Excelsior Springs, MO

ST LOUIS–1902: West Baden, French Lick, IN; 1903: Baton Rouge, LA; 1904: Corsicana, TX; 1905-06: Dallas, TX; 1907: San Antonio, TX; 1908: Shreveport, LA; 1909: Houston, TX

PHILADELPHIA–1901: (no trip); 1902: Charlotte, NC; 1903: Jacksonville, FL; 1904: Spartanburg, SC; 1905: Shreveport, Mobile, AL; 1906: Montgomery, AL; 1907: Marlin Springs, TX; 1908-09: New Orleans, LA

WASHINGTON–1901: Hampton, VA; 1902-04: (no trip); 1905: Hampton, VA; 1906: Charlottesville, VA; 1907-09: Galveston, TX

CLUB OWNERS AND EXECUTIVES

The owners of the major league baseball clubs at the turn of the century were very much like owners of today. Most of them had already become affluent from non-baseball enterprises and through their attained wealth were able to purchase their way into baseball. Like today's magnates, they were sharp businessmen who took an interest in baseball operations with the belief that they could reap profits from it. But, in truth, many of them were addicted to the sport and endured considerable losses or very modest gains just for the sake of being involved in the national game. Whatever their motives, they all wanted to win. As in any competitive sport, winning championships not only generated money at the gate, but also all the fringe benefits that took the form of adulation, ego-gratification, publicity, respect, etc. Although many of the owners typified the greedy "robber-barons" of the age, their status gave them a respected role in the community. Some were tyrannical, independent autocrats, especially among the National League club owners. The club owners in the American League were indebted to league founder Ban Johnson for their lofty status, and out of a dedication to the new league's survival, were more cooperative and subservient. The only club owner who was a pure product of baseball was Charles Comiskey of the Chicago American League team. Commy had been a star player for the St. Louis Browns of the 1880's, then became a successful manager for several teams. He worked his way up into the front office and became owner/president of the St. Paul franchise in Johnson's Western League in the late 1890's. The St. Paul club was then relocated to Chicago in the renamed American League of 1900. "The Old Roman," as Comiskey was called, turned out to be a shrewd businessman and one of the most successful team owners in the major leagues for three decades. Connie Mack was another executive (besides his role as field manager) who came up through the ranks of baseball to enjoy a long and noteworthy career as part owner of the Philadelphia Athletics. Athletics' owner Ben Shibe was no stranger to baseball, having a long reputation as a manufacturer of baseballs and other sports equipment prior to his entry into the game itself. Oddly enough, his partner in the sporting goods business was A.J. Reach, part owner of the cross-town Phillies. By no small coincidence, the Reach baseball was adopted in 1901 as the official ball of the American League.

Charles Comiskey, the "Old Roman," was a key figure in the survival of the fledgling American League. Although he did not always see eye-to-eye with League President Ban Johnson, he personally developed his White Sox organization into a solid franchise.

Ben Shibe parlayed a fortune in the manufacture of sports equipment into successful ownership of the Philadelphia Athletics.

Frank Navin, a minority stock-holder, became secretary/-business manager of the Detroit club. His active role in running the affairs of the team led to his rapid rise to principal owner in 1908.

John T. Brush sold his ownership of the Cincinnati club and took over the New York Giants operation in 1903. Brush fought the new AL tooth-and-nail and was instrumental in an undercover maneuver to disrupt the Baltimore club and recruit its star players, including John McGraw. He was easily the most disliked owner in major league baseball.

Front office titles varied from club to club and did not necessarily identify real power and responsibility. The general manager of today would claim the title of Secretary or Business Manager or both. Or, more likely, the club President, who may or may not be the principal owner, would be the top executive. Some individual owners, like Charles Comiskey, took a hand in all aspects of team operation, while others, like Bill Yawkey, stayed in the background and left the administrative duties and decisions in the hands of the Business Manager or Secretary. Secretary Frank Navin, only a limited stockholder in the Detroit organization, actually ran the club and soon became the principal owner when Yawkey lost interest. Cincinnati owner Garry Herrmann played a dual role as chairman of the National Commission and President of his own club, a delicate situation in view of potential conflict of interest. Herrmann, however, rose to the task and his integrity was never seriously challenged. Indeed, his close personal friendship with American League President Ban Johnson suggested a possibly unfair preference for AL interests rather than those of his own league. The harmony that existed among the American League owners was a marked contrast to the bickering, maneuvering, and feuding between some of the more headstrong NL owners. Reds' (and later Giants') owner John T. Brush plotted with disgruntled Baltimore Manager John McGraw behind the scenes in 1902, and deviously purchased controlling interest in the Baltimore club. The strategy was aimed at decimating the Orioles roster and releasing many star players over to the New York Giants, including McGraw himself. It was a mortal blow to the Baltimore operation and threatened to seriously undermine the infrastructure of the new league. Ban Johnson was able to ride out the storm by restocking the Oriole team, and the balance of the season schedule was played out as planned. AL baseball in Baltimore was doomed, but the American League's counter-strategy was to transfer the franchise to Brush's backyard, Manhattan, for the 1903 season. Popular New York City politician and businessman Joseph Gordon was the principal owner of the new American League "invaders," or "Highlanders" as they were appropriately labeled by the press.

While Garry Herrmann perhaps exemplified the benevolent and likable owner, the majority of National League clubs were run by selfish tyrants no more principled than the many "thugs" who played under them. John T. Brush managed to offend everyone at one time or another with his tactics, and when he transferred his interests to New York, he succeeded another bullheaded egotist in Andy Freedman. Charles Ebbets of Brooklyn and James Hart of Chicago were of the same cloth and the armistice with the American League in 1903 was accomplished over their general resistance (along with Brush, Freedman, and Soden of Boston). The Robison brothers in St. Louis were not among the players' favorite employers, as evidenced by the desertion of so many star players over to the AL Browns in 1902, never to return. It was not simply higher salary offers that attracted so many National Leaguers over to the new league, but the opportunity to play for ownership that was more even-handed and conciliatory in its dealings with players.

Garry Herrmann became president of the Cincinnati Reds after J. T. Brush sold out. Garry was well known and respected in the Queen City. He subsequently presided over the newly formed National Commission, which ran baseball after the AL/NL wars were settled.

ADMINISTRATION OF MAJOR LEAGUE BASEBALL

When the baseball war finally was settled by a peace agreement in early 1903 and the new American League was granted legitimacy as a rival major league, the novel task of administering two distinct leagues under a common body of rules had to be resolved. The new National Agreements called for a three-man executive panel under the title of the National Commission. Garry Herrmann of Cincinnati was elected to chair the commission and function as a "tie-breaker" for the two remaining members, the presidents of the two leagues—namely Ban Johnson and Harry Pulliam. With the bitter taste of war behind them, the commission served its purpose well and was able to establish policies and settle disputes in a fair and just manner in the ensuing years. Major league baseball was supervised by this "troika" arrangement well into the next decade, but finally transferred its authority to a lone commissioner after the Black Sox scandal of 1920.

LEAGUE EXECUTIVES

The administration of the new American League in its first decade (and indeed for future decades) can be simply defined by one name—Byron Bancroft "Ban" Johnson. Ban was no accident of history—he was a smart businessman with a keen knowledge of baseball and a genius for organization. He personally forged his minor Western League into a successful venture, and when the troubled National League was forced to reduce its membership from 12 to 8 clubs in 1900, he wisely determined that a second major league was a workable idea. He recruited a select group of well-heeled entrepreneurs and restructured his Western League with new franchises in the major league markets of Chicago and Cleveland, with planned clubs in the NL-vacated Eastern cities of Baltimore and Washington the following year. He renamed his circuit the American League and after the 1900 season, announced that his league would no longer be bound to the National Agreements and would henceforth seek major league status. Johnson shrewdly guided his new league through the bitter conflicts with the established league in the formative years. Once peace was restored and recognition was a fact of life, he participated in the newly formed National Commission and continued to command his new league through a decade of successful growth. He was also blessed with an able assistant, Secretary Robert McRoy, who took care of routine league matters throughout the decade.

The National League had no counterpart to Ban Johnson to lead them through the turmoil of the baseball wars and beyond. At the turn of the century, the destiny of the league was dictated by a handful of feudal club owners, a condition that actually paved the way for the establishment of the rival league. Nicholas "Nick" Young had emerged from the 19th century as a revered figurehead assuming the role of NL Secretary/President, but he had little authority to formulate league strategy against the invaders. Most of the resistance to the outlaw league came from the many lawsuits filed by individual NL clubs to prohibit contract jumping by their players. The most powerful and influential club owners—John T. Brush (Cincinnati, NY), Arthur H. Soden (Boston), and James A. Hart (Chicago), formed a body of three and assumed control of the league in 1901. Young was retained as League Secretary to carry out their bidding. They began to realize some victories in the courts, as the Pennsylvania Supreme Court ruled that Lajoie, Flick, Fraser, and Bernhard were forbidden to play for the AL Philadelphia Athletics. Legendary father figure to baseball A.G. Spalding was selected in late 1901 to be National League President, but it was still a ceremonial title and subservient to the three-man executive board. When an armistice appeared at hand in April 1902, Spalding stepped down and once again the league could not agree on a successor. Finally, Harry C. Pulliam of Pittsburgh was named to the post in December 1902. Pulliam was, however, no Ban Johnson and even though he remained at the helm through most of the decade, his tenure was uninspiring and wrought with frustration. Pulliam eventually suffered a nervous breakdown early in 1909, then stunned the baseball world in July of that year by committing suicide. John Heydler was named acting President to fill out Pulliam's term. Heydler was a well-qualified choice with a good baseball background—former baseball writer, umpire, and secretary-treasurer of the league under Pulliam. Heydler was replaced by former umpire Tom Lynch in December 1909 and then resumed the post of league secretary.

Baseball's National Commission in 1909, plus AL Secretary Robert McRoy on the far right. From the left, new NL President John Heydler, Garry Herrmann, and AL President Ban Johnson.

THE NATIONAL LEAGUE

Officials:

NICHOLAS E.
"NICK" YOUNG
President 1900-01
Secretary 1902

A. G.
SPALDING
Interim President
Late 1901-02

Executive Board 1902:

JOHN T.
BRUSH

ARTHUR H.
SODEN

JAMES
HART

Directors ('03-'04)
A. H. SODEN
JAMES HART
JOHN T. BRUSH
BARNEY DREYFUS

HARRY PULLIAM
President
Late 1902-Mid 1909

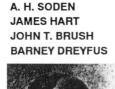

JOHN HEYDLER
Asst. Sec'y 1903-06
Sec'y/Treas 1907-09
Acting Pres. 1909

THOMAS LYNCH
President (Dec. 1909):

Umpires:

WILLIAM TERRY 1900
CYRUS "NED" SWARTWOOD 1900
THOMAS POWERS 1900-02
JOHN GAFFNEY 1900
CHARLES SNYDER 1900
TOM CONNOLLY 1900
BOB EMSLIE 1900-09
TIM HURST 1900, 1903-04
HANK O'DAY 1900-09
TOM BROWN 1900-02
FRANK DWYER 1900-01
HARRY COLGAN 1901, 1903
BILLY NASH 1901
ELMER CUNNINGHAM 1900-01
JOE CANTILLON 1902
ARLIE LATHAM 1900, 1902
ARTHUR IRWIN 1902
TOM LYNCH 1902
JIM JOHNSTONE 1903-09
GUS MORAN 1903-04
JAMES HOLLIDAY 1903
FRANK PEARS 1903-07
CHIEF ZIMMER 1904-05
CHARLES KENNEDY 1904-06
JOHN STAFFORD 1904
WM. CARPENTER 1904, 1906-07
BILL KLEM 1905-09
GEORGE BAUSWINE 1905, 1908
JEREMIAH MURRAY 1905
? SUPPLE 1906
JOHN CONWAY 1906
STEPHEN KANE 1906, 1909
CHARLES RIGLER 1906-09
FRANCIS RUDDERHAM 1907-08
CLARENCE OWENS 1908-09
STEVE CUSACK 1909
HARRY TRUBY 1909
BILL BRENNAN 1909

HANK O'DAY

TIM
HURST

BOB EMSLIE

JIM JOHNSTONE

BILL KLEM

WILLIAM
CARPENTER

CHARLES RIGLER

THE AMERICAN LEAGUE

Officials:

BYRON BANCROFT "BAN" JOHNSON
President 1900-1909

CHARLES W. SOMERS
Vice President

ROBERT McROY
Secretary

Umpires:

WILLIAM TERRY 1901
JACK SHERIDAN 1901-09
TOM CONNOLLY 1901-09
JOE CANTILLON 1901
JOHN HASKELL 1901
AL MANASSAU 1901
WILLIAM BETTS 1901, 1903
WILLIAM HART 1901
JIM JOHNSTONE 1902
FRANK "SILK" O'LAUGHLIN 1902-09
BOB CARRUTHERS 1902-03
JAMES HASSETT 1903
FRANK PEARS 1903
JOHN KERINS 1903
JOHN ADAMS 1903
JOHN "JACK" EGAN 1903, 1907-09
FRANK DWYER 1904
CHARLES KING 1904
WILLIAM CARPENTER 1904
JOHN McCARTHY 1905
TOM KELLY 1905
TIM HURST 1905-09
TOM CONNOR 1905-06
ERNEST QUIGLEY 1906
BILLY EVANS 1906-09
JOHN STAFFORD 1907
JOHN KERIN 1908-09
FRED PERRINE 1909
BILL DINNEEN 1909

JACK SHERIDAN

TOM CONNOLLY

"SILK" O'LAUGHLIN

BILLY EVANS

TIM HURST

BALTIMORE 1901-1902

POPULATION: (1900) 509,000

City Hall, Baltimore, Md.

City Hall

Washington Monument, Mt. Vernon M. E. Church and Hotel Stafford, Baltimore, Md.

Washington Monument, Hotel Stafford, Mt. Vernon M.E. Church

THE NEWSPAPERS

THE BASEBALL REPORTERS

JOE CUMMINGS *News*

JOHN H. ANDERSON *Herald*
SAMUEL C. APPLEBY *Sun*
FRANK E. PATTERSON *Sun*

BALTIMORE American League Park 1901-02

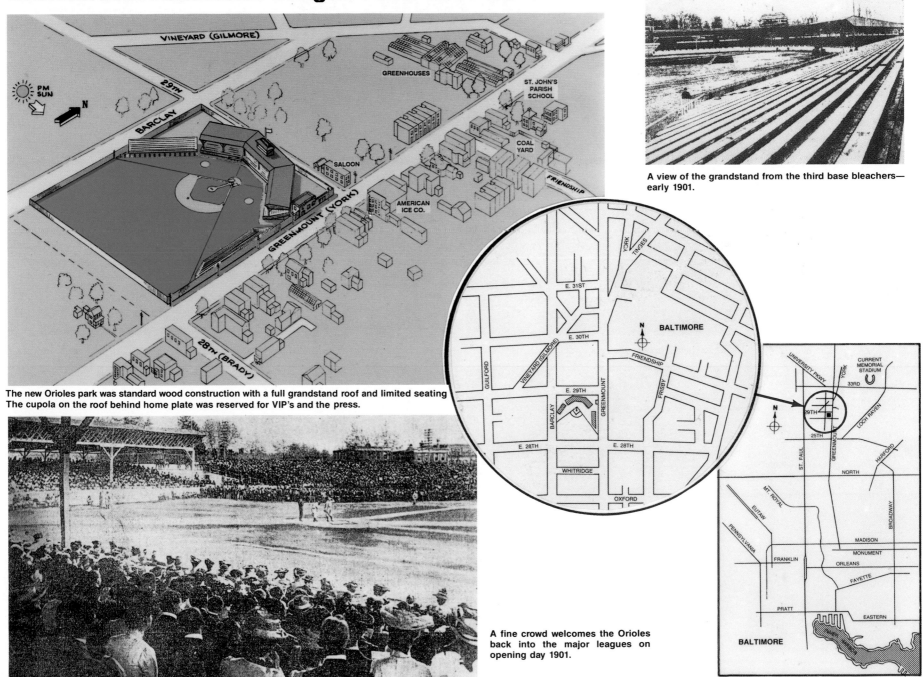

A view of the grandstand from the third base bleachers—early 1901.

The new Orioles park was standard wood construction with a full grandstand roof and limited seating. The cupola on the roof behind home plate was reserved for VIP's and the press.

A fine crowd welcomes the Orioles back into the major leagues on opening day 1901.

BOSTON 1900-1909

POPULATION: (1900) 561,000
(1910) 670,000

Commonwealth Avenue

Copley Square and Trinity Church

Tremont Street

The Boston Common and State House

BOSTON 1900-1909 (continued)

THE NEWSPAPERS

SCORE OF THE GREATEST BASEBALL GAME EVER PLAYED

THE BASEBALL REPORTERS

WALTER S. BARNES, Jr.
Journal, Herald

JACOB C. MORSE
Herald, Sporting Life correspondent

OS W. BROWN
Traveler

TIM MURNANE
Globe

T. J. BURKE
Journal

HERMAN NICKERSON
Herald, Journal

SAMUEL P. CARRICK
Post

PAUL SHANNON
Post

ARTHUR D. COOPER
Post

AL E. WATTS
Traveler

RALPH E. McMILLAN
Herald

WALLACE GOLDSMITH
cartoonist
Herald, Globe

BILL BAILEY *Post*
ARTHUR BARRETT
CARL BARRETT *Record*
IRVING S. CLARK *American*
LOUIS A. DOUGHER *Traveller*
ARTHUR DUFFY *Post*
BOB DUNBAR *Journal, Post*
W. F. "FRANK" EATON *Record*
FRANCIS A. FROST *Record*
CARL GREEN *Record*
PETER F. KELLEY *Journal*
GORDON MACKAY *Journal*
? MAHER *Journal*
ARTHUR McPHERSON *Journal*
ALBERT W. C. "BERT" MITCHELL *American*
FRED P. O'CONNELL *Post*
JAMES O'CONNELL *Globe*
E. J. O'CONNOR *Post*
JOHN R. ROBINSON *Traveler*
BILLY ROSS *American*
J. L. SULLIVAN *American*
MYRON W. TOWNSEND *Traveller, Post*
MELVILLE E. WEBB Jr. *Globe*

artists/cartoonists:
? DOWLING *Post*
H. G. LASKEY *Globe*
? "NORMAN" *Post*

C.E. BEANE
editor-in-chief

JACOB C. MORSE
editor

BOSTON

**American League . . .
HUNTINGTON AVENUE GROUNDS 1901-1909**

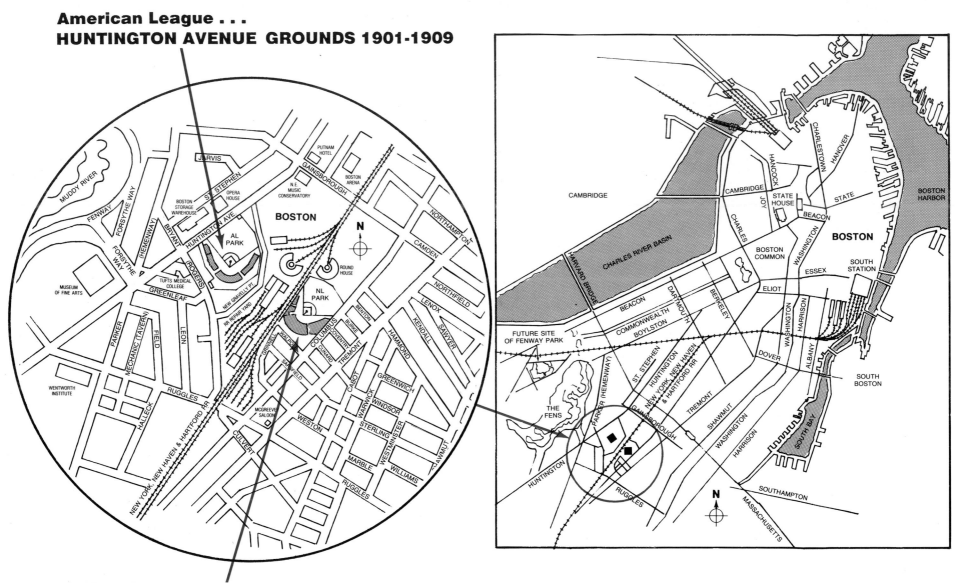

**National League . . .
SOUTH END GROUNDS 1900-1909**

BOSTON American League . . . HUNTINGTON AVENUE GROUNDS 1901-1909

This panoramic view from the left field corner shows the vast acreage of the new Boston AL grounds. Plenty of standing room without severely restricting the playing field dimensions.

The grandstand and main entrance of the Huntington Ave. grounds as seen from Rogers Ave., looking east.

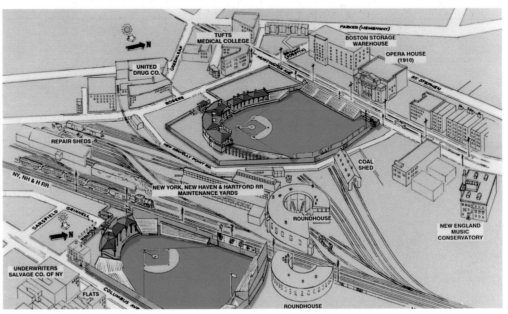

The two Boston baseball parks after 1900 were the closest neighbors in the big leagues—only the railroad tracks and yards separated them.

BOSTON American League . . . HUNTINGTON AVENUE GROUNDS 1901-1909

A view of the grandstand and first base bleachers from the right field corner.

A rooftop view of straightaway center field, with the left field fence paralleling Huntington Avenue.

Boston's "royal rooters" were provided with "on the field" accommodations in front of the main grandstand for big games.

BOSTON National League . . . SOUTH END GROUNDS 1900-1909

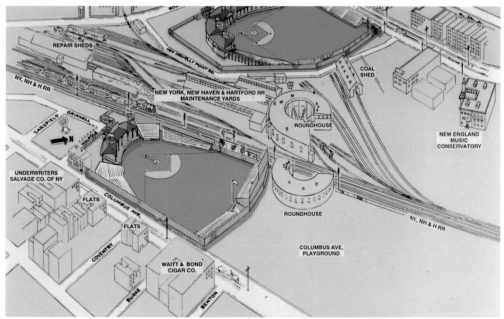

A view of the main entrance and grandstand from Walpole Avenue.

The Boston Nationals field was cramped for space, hopelessly wedged in between the railroad tracks and Columbus Avenue.

Full bleachers on both sides of the center field flag pole provided much needed extra seats by 1910.

BROOKLYN 1900-1909

POPULATION: (1900) 1,167,000
(1910) 1,679,000

The famous Brooklyn Bridge

Fulton & Washington Sts. from Borough Hall

THE NEWSPAPERS

THE BROOKLYN DAILY EAGLE.

FOUR O'CLOCK.   NEW YORK CITY, THURSDAY, APRIL 12, 1906.—VOL. 67, NO. 101.—80 PAGES INCLUDING PICTURE SECTION.   THREE C'␣

VESUVIUS SEEMS | | SUNNY SKIES FOR OPENING | | DR. MYERS TO DEFY POLICE | | CASTRO'S RESIGNATIO

The Brooklyn Citizen.

VOL. XXXIII.—NO. 94.   BROOKLYN, SUNDAY, APRIL 5, 1903.—TWENTY-FOUR PAGES.   PRICE THREE CENTS.

THE STANDARD UNION   DAILY ONE CENT.

Fair and Colder To-morrow.

VOL. XLI. NO. 281.   BROOKLYN, TUESDAY, APRIL 11, 1905.   TWELVE PAGES

FOUR O'CLOCK EDITION. | MORSE JOINS LORD | RUSSIANS SEEK | EIGHT MINISTERS | MANY BILLS RUSHED THROUGH

(BROOKLYN TIMES)

THE BASEBALL REPORTERS

ABE YAGER
Eagle,
Sporting News correspondent

L. F. WOOSTER
Times

WM. J. GRANGER *Citizen*
WM. A. RAFTER *Standard Union*
THOMAS RICE *Eagle*

artists:
FRANK DUNHAM *Eagle*
NELSON HARDING *Eagle*

BROOKLYN National League . . . WASHINGTON PARK 1900-1909

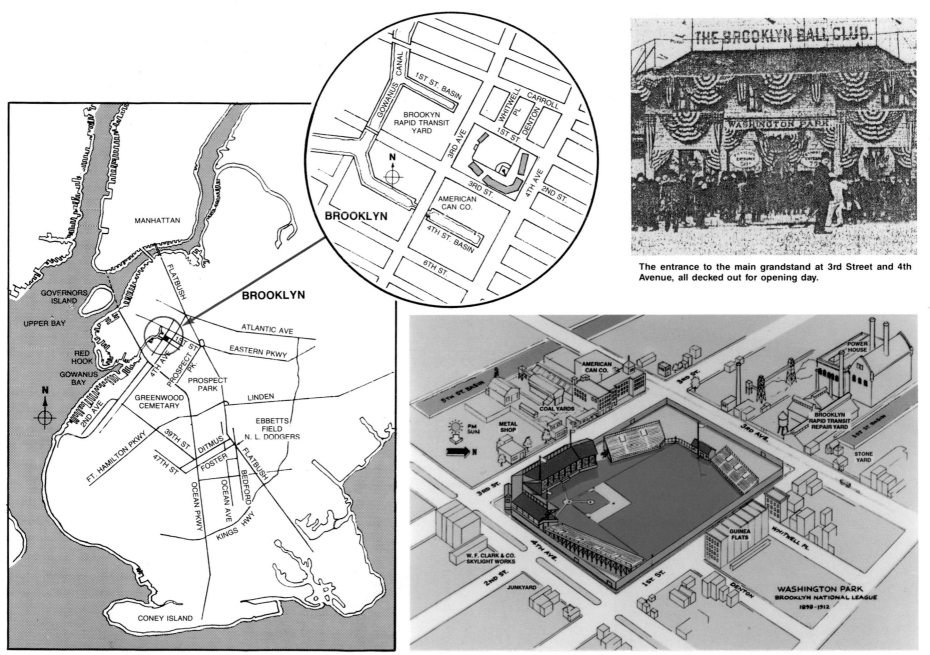

The entrance to the main grandstand at 3rd Street and 4th Avenue, all decked out for opening day.

Washington Park, which opened in 1898, was the successor to an earlier Washington Park baseball facility that was roughly "catty-corner" from this ball field.

BROOKLYN National League . . . WASHINGTON PARK 1900-1909

A ground level shot from left field, with a good view of the first base bleachers and grandstand.

The bleacher entrance at 3rd Avenue and First Street. Note the 3rd Ave. trolley tracks and cobblestones.

A view looking down the right field wall along 1st Street. The Guinea Flats apartments overlooked the right field fence and provided residents with a fine view of the game—a source of irritation for the Brooklyn management. Many devices were used to obstruct and frustrate these "freeloaders" over the years.

The champion Brooklyns working out at Washington Park at the 1900 season opener. The view is looking toward the left field corner.

CHICAGO 1900-1909

POPULATION: (1900) 1,700,000
(1910) 2,185,000

The famous stockyards, South Side

Michigan Avenue looking north

The Chicago River & Van Buren St. Bridge

Lake Shore Drive

CHICAGO 1900-1909 (continued)

THE NEWSPAPERS

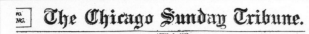

THE BASEBALL REPORTERS

JAMES CRUISINBERRY
Record-Herald

RING LARDNER
Examiner, Tribune

IRVING E. "SY" SANBORN
Tribune, Sporting News correspondent

CHARLES DRYDEN
American, Tribune

MALCOLM MACLEAN
Chronicle, Record-Herald

RICHARD TOBIN
Inter-Ocean

HUGH FULLERTON
Tribune, Examiner

JESSE MATTESON
Chronicle, American

WILLIAM E. VEECK
American

JAMES GILRUTH
Daily News

W. A. "BILLY" PHELAN
Journal

ED WESTLAKE
Post

FRED HEWITT
Inter-Ocean

GEORGE RICE
Daily News, Journal

HARVEY WOODRUFF
Record-Herald, Tribune

CHARLES "JESSE" HUGHES
Record-Herald

FRANK HUTCHINSON
Inter-Ocean

H. D. JOHNSON
Record-Herald

G. W. AXELSON *Record-Herald*
R. C. CORNELL *Journal, Examiner*
MARK W. CRESAP *Record-Herald*
HARRY DANIEL *Inter-Ocean*
C. E. DUNKLEY *Inter-Ocean*
FRANK X. FINNEGAN *Chronicle, Examiner*
HARRY W. FORD *Inter-Ocean*
C. D. HAGERTY *Associated Press*
FRED HAYNER *Daily News*
THOMAS HYNES *Examiner*

HUGH KEOUGH (HEK) *Tribune*
GEORGE A. MACDONALD *Journal*
JOHN M. MAXWELL *American, Inter-Ocean*
STACEY MOSSER *Record-Herald*
JOE MURPHY *Tribune*
E. S. SHERIDAN *Tribune*
ED SMITH *Chronicle*
JACK TANNER *Inter-Ocean*
JOE VILA *Tribune*

artists/cartoonists:
? TAYLOR *Daily News*
DON WILSON *Record-Herald*

CHICAGO 1900-1909 (continued)

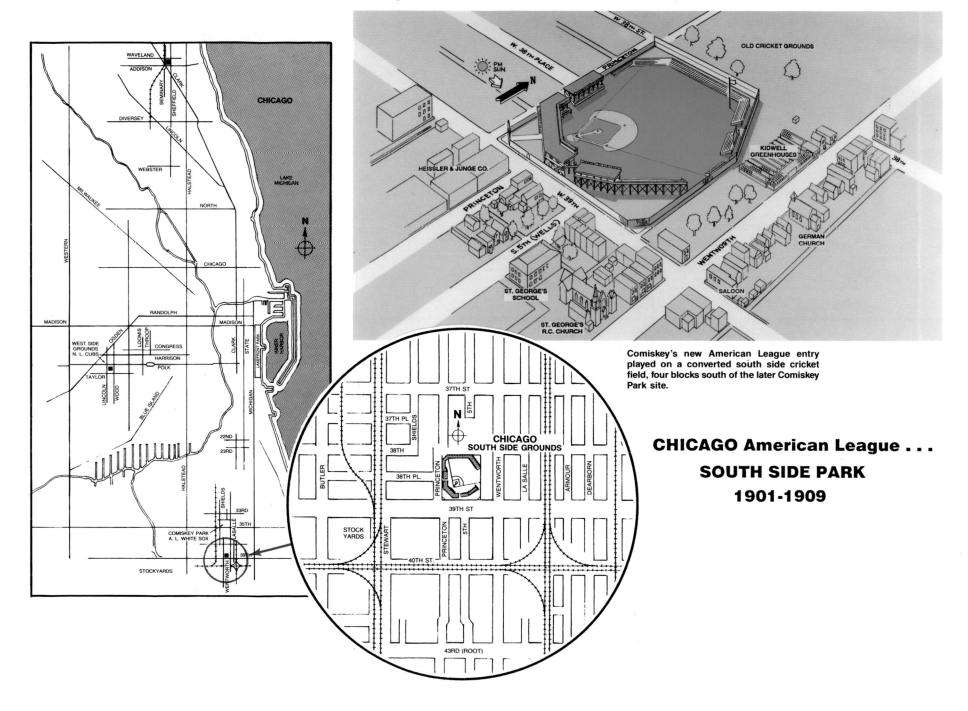

Comiskey's new American League entry played on a converted south side cricket field, four blocks south of the later Comiskey Park site.

CHICAGO American League . . .

SOUTH SIDE PARK

1901-1909

CHICAGO American League . . . SOUTH SIDE PARK 1901-1909

A fine view from left field of a 1904 game vs. Boston.

The main entrance at the southwest corner of the grounds.

A game action scene from a City Series game with the cross-town National Leaguers.

CHICAGO National League . . . WEST SIDE GROUNDS 1900-1909

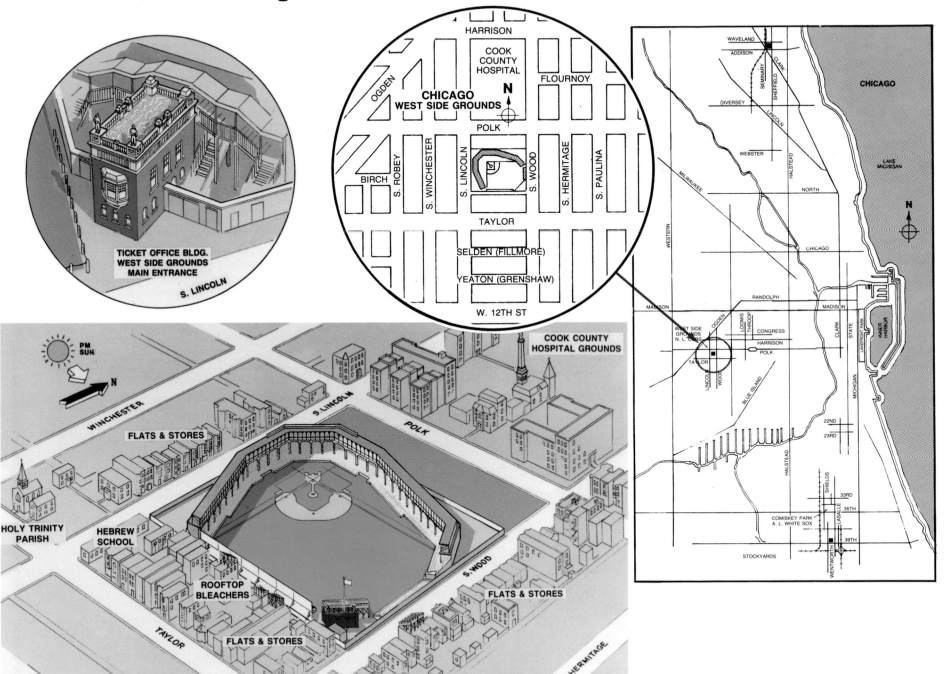

TICKET OFFICE BLDG.
WEST SIDE GROUNDS
MAIN ENTRANCE

S. LINCOLN

CHICAGO
WEST SIDE GROUNDS

N

HARRISON

COOK
COUNTY
HOSPITAL

FLOURNOY

OGDEN

POLK

BIRCH

S. ROBEY

S. WINCHESTER

S. LINCOLN

S. WOOD

S. HERMITAGE

S. PAULINA

TAYLOR

SELDEN (FILLMORE)

YEATON (GRENSHAW)

W. 12TH ST

CHICAGO

LAKE
MICHIGAN

WAVELAND
ADDISON
SEMINARY
SHEFFIELD
CLARK
DIVERSEY
LINCOLN
WEBSTER
HALSTEAD
NORTH
MILWAUKEE
WESTERN
CHICAGO
RANDOLPH
MADISON
MADISON
CLARK
STATE
LAKEFRONT PARK
INNER HARBOR
OGDEN
LOOMIS
THROOP
CONGRESS
WEST SIDE
GROUNDS
N. L. CUBS
HARRISON
POLK
TAYLOR
LINCOLN
WOOD
BLUE ISLAND
MICHIGAN
HALSTEAD
22ND
23RD
SHIELDS
33RD
35TH
COMISKEY PARK
A. L. WHITE SOX
LASALLE
39TH
WENTWORTH
STOCKYARDS

PM
SUN

N

WINCHESTER

S. LINCOLN

POLK

COOK COUNTY
HOSPITAL GROUNDS

FLATS & STORES

HOLY TRINITY
PARISH

HEBREW
SCHOOL

ROOFTOP
BLEACHERS

S. WOOD

FLATS & STORES

TAYLOR

FLATS & STORES

S. HERMITAGE

The West Side Grounds was bordered on the north by Cook County Hospital. The glory years of Cubs baseball took place here.

CHICAGO National League . . . WEST SIDE GROUNDS 1900-1909

A panorama of the park taken at a big game late in the decade shows the full sweep of the roofed upper deck.

The original grandstand as it appeared early in the decade.

The new center field club house under construction in 1905.

A view along the right field fence showing the "wildcat" bleachers that cropped up on rooftops adjacent to the outfield fences.

A ground level view of the magnificent main entrance building, replete with rooftop statuary erected in 1908.

CINCINNATI 1900-1909

POPULATION: (1900) 326,000
(1910) 365,000

Fifth Street, downtown

Suspension Bridge and city skyline

THE NEWSPAPERS

SPORTING | THE COMMERCIAL TRIBUNE. | FICTION
CINCINNATI | PAGES 11 TO 20. | APRIL 12, 1908.
SILK O'LOUGHLIN CALLING HIS CELEBRATED "STRIKE TUH" AND MIKE MITCHELL CROSSING FIRST BASE.

THE CINCINNATI ENQUIRER.
MAIN SHEET SIXTEEN PAGES.
SUNDAY MORNING, APRIL 15, 1906.
IL PANIC IN CHURCH | ASKED | DEATH FOLLOWS EXPLOSION ON BIG BATTLI

TIMES-STAR'S CIRCULATION *IS GREATER THAN TWICE THE COMBINED CIRCULATION* OF ALL OTHER
7TH THE CINCINNATI TIMES-STAR.
SIX CENTS A WEEK | CINCINNATI, FRIDAY, JUNE 1, 190 | ONE CENT A COPY

Weather | SIX O'CLOCK—BASEBALL | 10 Pages
BASEBALL | THE CINCINNATI POST | SPORTING
VOL. 23. NO. 44. | CINCINNATI, SATURDAY, AUGUST 20, 1906. | PRICE ONE CENT.

THE BASEBALL REPORTERS

J. ED GRILLO
*Commercial
Tribune*

FRANK W.
ROSTOCK
Post

HARRY WELDON
Enquirer

REN MULFORD Jr.
*Post,
Sporting Life
correspondent*

FRED J.
HEWITT
Post

JACK RYDER
Enquirer

CHARLES W.
MURPHY
Enquirer

F. W. FORSYTHE *Sporting Life correspondent*
JIM C. HAMILTON *Commercial Tribune*
W. A. "BILLY" PHELAN *Post, Times-Star*
ROSS TENNEY *Post, Enquirer*
MYRON TOWNSEND *Commercial Tribune, Times-Star*
CHARLES H. ZUBER *Times-Star, Sporting News correspondent*

photographers:
F. BOELLINGER *Commercial Tribune*
CHARLES BURROUGHS *Times-Star*
J. R. SCHMIDT *Commercial Tribune*

artists/cartoonists:
? SHAFER *Enquirer*

DETROIT American League . . . BENNETT PARK 1901-1909

In 1903, the playing field was totally resurfaced along with new bleacher construction and modifications to the roofed grandstand.

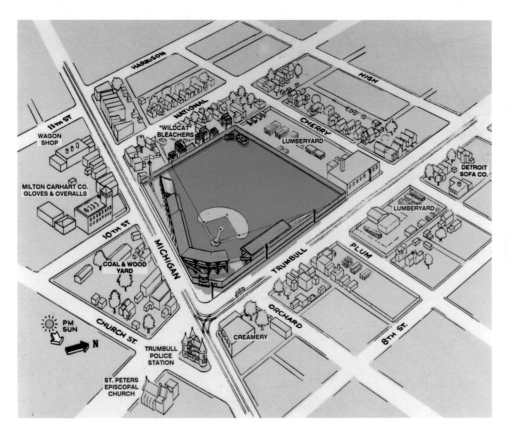

The corner of Michigan & Trumbull prior to opening game 1901—the first big league contest for the Motor City in the twentieth century.

The park dated back to 1896, and the site of Michigan & Trumbull Avenues is the oldest continuous location of major league baseball. The current Tiger Stadium still occupies the same real estate.

DETROIT American League . . . BENNETT PARK 1901-1909

Another view of the main entrance as it appeared about 1910.

The main grandstand late in the decade. Tubular steel roof supports improved the field view for spectators.

The famous "wildcat" bleachers that sprung up in back yards behind the left field fence.

Detroit management repeatedly made attempts to obstruct the view from the "wildcat" stands. This view of the left field area shows canvas strips used in the 1909 World Series.

MILWAUKEE 1901

POPULATION: (1900) 285,000

Milwaukee River, downtown

THE NEWSPAPERS

THE BASEBALL REPORTERS

TOM ANDREWS *Evening Wisconsin*
H. H. COHN
ARTHUR B. MARSH
TED SULLIVAN *Evening Wisconsin*

Grand Ave., looking west

City Hall

Prospect Avenue

MILWAUKEE American League . . . LLOYD STREET GROUNDS 1901

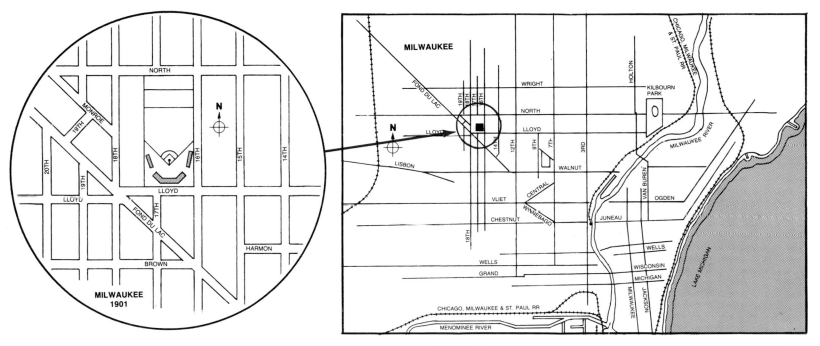

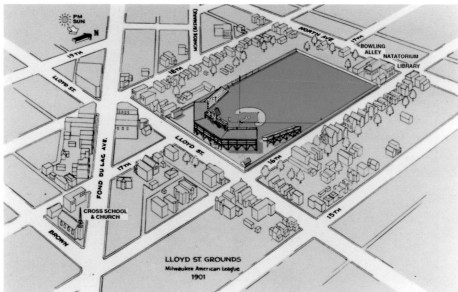

Lloyd Street Grounds had limited seating, but the team's lackluster 1901 performance negated the prospect of a sizable fan following.

Some rare views, possibly the only photographs of Milwaukee's ill-fated major league arena.

NEW YORK 1900-1909

POPULATION (MANHATTAN):
(1900) 1,850,000
(1910) 2,365,000

MADISON SQUARE AND METROPOLITAN BUILDING, NEW YORK CITY.

Metropolitan Bldg. and Madison Square

Madison Square from the Flatiron Bldg.

SPEEDWAY, NEW YORK.

The Harlem River Speedway, north of the Polo Grounds

Wall Street

FLATIRON BUILDING, BROADWAY & 23RD STREET, NEW YORK.

Flatiron Bldg., Broadway & 23rd

NEW YORK 1900-1909 (continued)

THE NEWSPAPERS

photographers:

? STEFANO *Telegram*

CHARLES CONLON
World, Telegram

THE BASEBALL REPORTERS

BOZEMAN BULGER *World*

W. J. McBETH *American*

GEORGE TIDDEN *World*

J. N. WHEELER *Herald*

SAM CRANE *Journal, American*

SID MERCER *Globe*

GEORGE E. FIRSTBROOK *Mail*

HARRY NIEMEYER *World, Telegram, Globe*

JOHN B. "JACK" FOSTER *Herald, Telegram*

W. A. "BILLY" PHELAN *Telegraph*

J. J. KARPF *Times, Mail*

JOHN POLLOCK *World*

WM. F. KIRK *American, Journal*

JAMES PRICE *Press*

PURVES KNOX *Mail, Sun*

W. M. RANKIN *Clipper, Sporting News*

WILLIAM F. KOELSTH *Sporting Life correspondent*

MARK ROTH *Globe*

W. W. AULICK *Mail, Times*
SAM AUSTIN *Herald, Police Gazette*
FRED BARBER *Times*
J. BENEFIELD *Times*
O. P. CAYLOR
CHARLES CRANE *Press*
ERNEST CROWHURST *Times*
GEORGE DALY *Tribune*
PETE DONOHUE *World*
W. B. "BILLY" HANNA *Press, Sun*
W. H. HICKS *Journal*
JIM KENNEDY *Times*
W. J. LAMPTON *Times*
ERNEST J. LANIGAN *Press*
TOM LEWIS *Telegraph*
JOHN MANDIGO *Sun*
CHARLES MATHISON *Globe*
J. W. McCONNAUGHEY *American & Journal, Examiner*
GEORGE McCURDY *Times*
JOE McGINN
DAN MILLS
GYM PAGLEY *World*
JOHN D. PRINGLE *Daily News*
NORMAN ROSE *United Press*
ALAN SANGREE *American & Journal, Globe*
HARRY SCHUMACHER *Mail*
LYNDON SMITH *World*
GEORGE STACKHOUSE *Tribune*
W. J. SULLIVAN *American & Journal*
CHARLES SUMMERVILLE *American & Journal*
C. E. VAN LOAN *American & Journal*
JOE VILA *Sun, Sporting News correspondent*
W. A. WOLFE *Tribune*

artists/cartoonists:

R. EDGREN
American & Journal
GEORGE HERRIMAN
American & Journal
J. NORMAN LYND
Herald
? SINCLAIR *Telegram*
? WARREN *Telegram*
WINDSOR M. ? *Herald*

NEW YORK 1900-1909 (continued)

American League . . . HILLTOP PARK 1903-1909

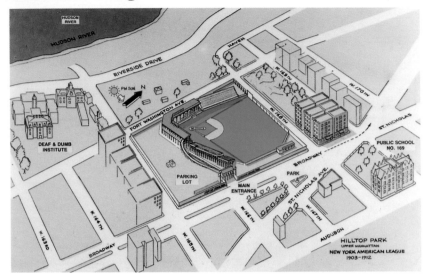

HILLTOP PARK
UPPER MANHATTAN
NEW YORK AMERICAN LEAGUE
1903-1912

National League . . . POLO GROUNDS 1900-1909

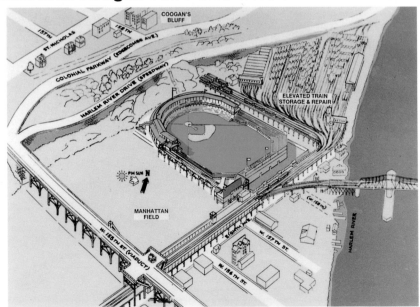

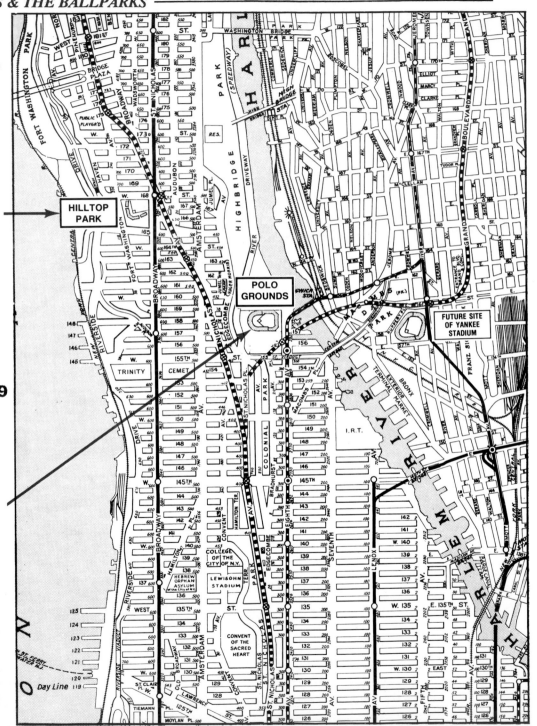

NEW YORK American League . . . HILLTOP PARK 1903-1909

An opening day crowd fills the grandstand and first base bleachers about midway through the decade.

The main entrance to the park, facing Broadway. The first base bleachers are visible on the right.

Opening day 1903—the first American League contest at the new Washington Heights facility. The grandstand roof is not yet in place, but it was a perfectly balmy spring day and the Highlanders defeated Washington 6-2.

A view of the first base bleachers, looking east toward the right field corner.

A sweeping panoramic view of Hilltop Park on Memorial Day 1910.

ST. LOUIS 1900-1909

**POPULATION: (1900) 575,000
(1910) 687,000**

Riverfront from Eads Bridge

THE NEWSPAPERS

THE BASEBALL REPORTERS

RICHARD J. COLLINS
Republic

JAMES A. CRUISINBERRY
Post-Dispatch

BRICE HOSKINS
Star

WILLIS E. JOHNSON
Globe-Democrat

W. E. KELSOE
Post-Dispatch

HAROLD W. LANIGAN
Globe-Democrat, Times

W. G. "BILLY" MURPHY
Post-Dispatch, Star, Sporting Life correspondent

MARION F. PARKER
Globe-Democrat

J. B. SHERIDAN
Post-Dispatch, Republic

MYRON TOWNSEND
Star-Chronicle

JOHN E. WRAY
Globe-Democrat, Post-Dispatch

JOE CAMPBELL *Chronicle*
W. J. COCHRANE *Post-Dispatch*
LOUIS DUFFY *Globe-Democrat*
W. B. FINNEY *Star*
A. J. FLANNER *Post-Dispatch, Globe-Democrat, News*
SIDNEY KEENER *Times*
CLARENCE LLOYD *Times*
CHARLEY McSKIMMING *Star*
E. L. MOCKLER *Globe-Democrat*
W. M. O'CONNOR *Globe-Democrat*
VICTOR PARRISH *Republic*
OLLIE VAUGHAN *Globe-Democrat*

artists/cartoonists:
? COLEMAN *Republic*
ED EKS *Globe-Democrat*
? KNOTT *Post-Dispatch*
H. B. MARTIN *Post-Dispatch*
S. CARLYLE MARTIN *Post-Dispatch*

ALFRED H. SPINK

CHARLES C. SPINK
publisher

JOSEPH M. CUMMINGS
editor

A. S. "JOE" FLANNER
editor

correspondents:
GEORGE GEER
ERNEST J. LANIGAN
CHARLES W. MEARS
BILLY MURPHY

ST. LOUIS (continued)

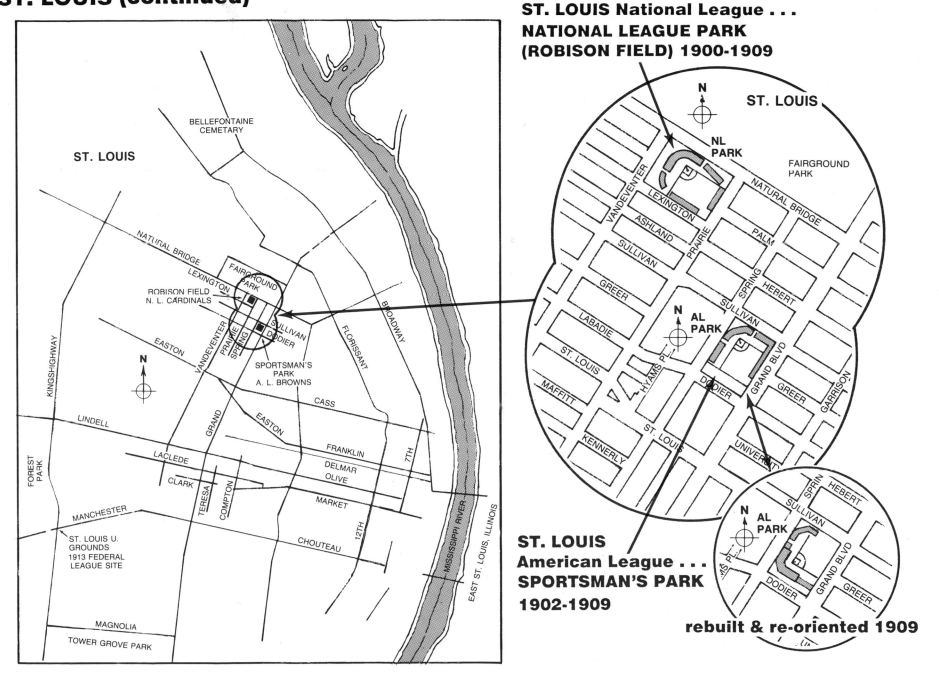

ST. LOUIS National League . . .
NATIONAL LEAGUE PARK
(ROBISON FIELD) 1900-1909

ST. LOUIS

N

NL PARK

FAIRGROUND PARK

VANDEVENTER

LEXINGTON

ASHLAND

PRAIRIE

NATURAL BRIDGE

PALM

SULLIVAN

SPRING

HEBERT

GREER

SULLIVAN

N

AL PARK

LABADIE

HYAMS PL.

DODIER

GRAND BLVD

GREER

GARRISON

ST. LOUIS

MAFFITT

ST. LOUIS

UNIVERSIT

KENNERLY

ST. LOUIS
American League . . .
SPORTSMAN'S PARK
1902-1909

SPRIN

HEBERT

SULLIVAN

N

AL PARK

HYAMS PL.

DODIER

GRAND BLVD

GREER

rebuilt & re-oriented 1909

ST. LOUIS

BELLEFONTAINE CEMETARY

NATURAL BRIDGE

LEXINGTON

FAIRGROUND PARK

ROBISON FIELD
N. L. CARDINALS

VANDEVENTER

PRAIRIE

SPRING

SULLIVAN

DODIER

SPORTSMAN'S PARK
A. L. BROWNS

BROADWAY

FLORISSANT

KINGSHIGHWAY

EASTON

N

CASS

LINDELL

GRAND

EASTON

FRANKLIN

7TH

FOREST PARK

LACLEDE

DELMAR

OLIVE

CLARK

TERESA

COMPTON

MARKET

MANCHESTER

ST. LOUIS U.
GROUNDS
1913 FEDERAL
LEAGUE SITE

12TH

CHOUTEAU

MISSISSIPPI RIVER

EAST ST. LOUIS, ILLINOIS

MAGNOLIA

TOWER GROVE PARK

ST. LOUIS National League . . .
NATIONAL LEAGUE PARK (ROBISON FIELD) 1900-1909

A scene in 1901 with "Pop" Schriver at the bat. The old roofed grandstand had limited seating but huge bleachers around the field compensated.

A view from the grandstand behind first base.

The main entrance at the corner of Vandeventer & Natural Bridge.

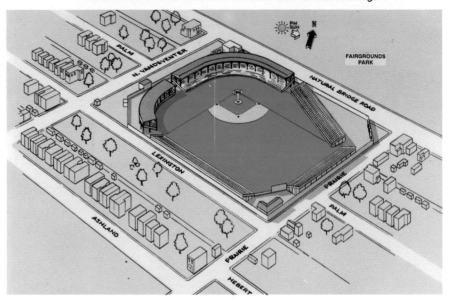

A wider view of a game in progress—probably around 1910.

ST. LOUIS American League . . . SPORTSMAN'S PARK 1902-1909

A panorama of the old main grandstand and first base pavilion that served the Browns through the 1908 season.

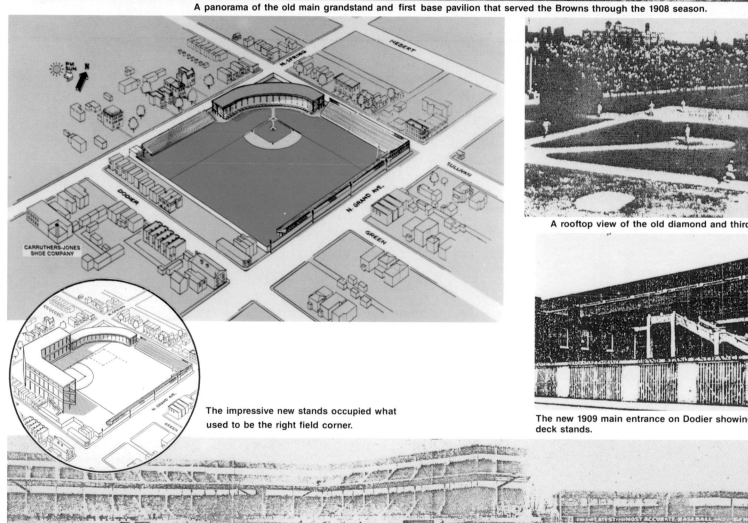

A rooftop view of the old diamond and third base bleachers—about 1903.

The impressive new stands occupied what used to be the right field corner.

The new 1909 main entrance on Dodier showing stairway ramps to the new upper deck stands.

WASHINGTON D.C. 1901-1909

POPULATION: (1900) 279,000
(1910) 331,000

The Mall, looking east from Washington Monument

THE NEWSPAPERS

The U.S. Patent Office

THE BASEBALL REPORTERS

PAUL W. EATON
Sporting Life correspondent

J. ED GRILLO
Post

THOMAS NOYES
Star

JOE CAMPBELL *Post*
JOHN A. DUGAN *Post*
HARRY H. FRY *Star*
JOHN HEYDLER *Sporting Life correspondent*
J. R. HILDEBRAND *Times*
GEORGE McCURDY *Post*
THOMAS S. RICE *Times*

WASHINGTON American League . . .

LEAGUE PARK (Florida Ave. NE) 1901-1903

LEAGUE PARK (7th St. NW) 1904-1909

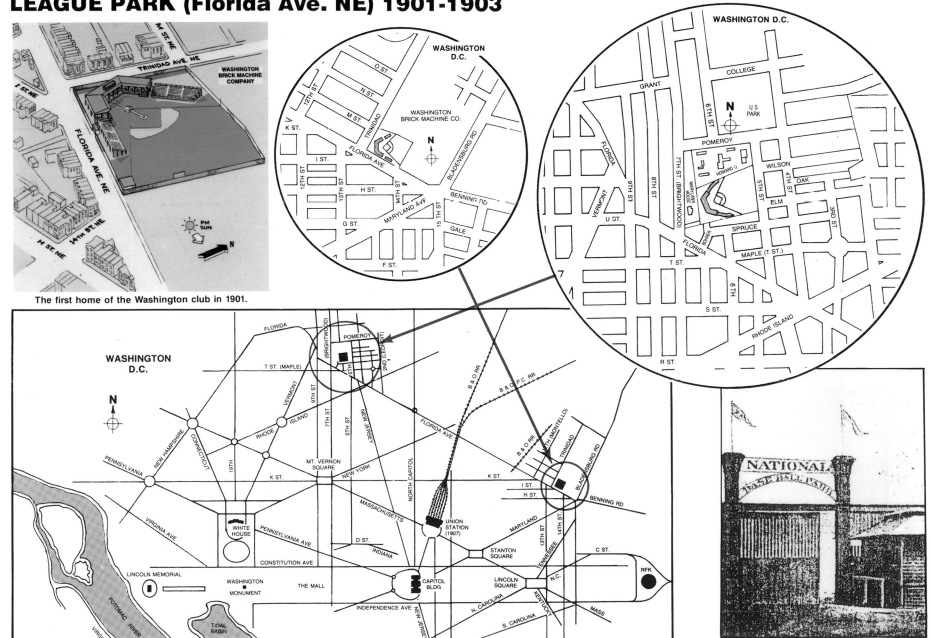

The first home of the Washington club in 1901.

The main entrance of the 1904-09 park, which was set back from 7th Street on the west.

BALTIMORE American League 1901-1902 (continued)

PLAYERS:

JACK DUNN
pitcher, infielder
1901

JIM JACKSON
outfielder 1901

FRANK FOREMAN
pitcher 1901-02

HARRY HOWELL
pitcher, utility
1901-02

ROGER BRESNAHAN
utility 1901-02

FRED SCHMIT
pitcher 1901

1901
ROAD

JOE McGINNITY
pitcher 1901-02

JAMES B. "CY" SEYMOUR
outfielder 1901-02

WILBERT ROBINSON
catcher 1901-02
(co-captain, mgr.-late 1902)

STEVE BRODIE
outfielder
1901

BILLY KEISTER
shortstop 1901

MIKE DONLIN
first base, outfield
1901

JOHN McGRAW
third baseman 1901-02
(manager 1901-mid 1902)

JIMMY WILLIAMS
infielder 1901-02

BALTIMORE American League 1901-1902 (continued)

PLAYERS:

CHARLES S. SHIELDS
pitcher, outfield 1902

ALBERT "KIP" SELBACH
outfielder 1902

"LONG TOM" HUGHES
pitcher 1902

Some 1902 Orioles. STANDING (L to R): Shields, Gilbert, Oyler, Sheckard. KNEELING (L to R): Selbach, McGann, Hughes.

I. I. MATHISON
infielder 1902

LEWIS D. "SNAKE" WILTSE
pitcher, utility 1902

TOM JONES
first, second base 1902

BILLY GILBERT
shortstop 1902

JOE KELLEY
utility 1902
(co-captain 1902)

1902
HOME

DAN McGANN
first baseman 1902

HERM McFARLAND
outfielder 1902

**ALEXANDER
"BROADWAY ALEC"
SMITH**
utility 1902

ISAAC "IKE" BUTLER
pitcher, outfield 1902

ANDY OYLER
infielder 1902

JOHN KATOLL
pitcher, outfielder 1902

HARRY ARNDT
utility 1902

BOSTON American League . . . . AMERICANS, RED SOX

OWNERS & OFFICERS:

CHARLES W. SOMERS
owner, president
1901-02

HENRY KILLILEA
owner, president
1903

directors (1901):
JIMMY COLLINS
D. J. HEARN
J. C. PELLETIER

business mgr.:
JOSEPH H. GAVIN ('01-02)
JOSEPH SMART ('03)

secretary/treasurer:
D. J. HEARN 1903

president (1902):
J. C. PELLETIER

attorney (1901): **MICHAEL J. MOORE**

JOHN I. TAYLOR
owner, president
1904-09-

CARL M. GREEN
treasurer,
business manager
1904-05

HUGH McBREEN
asst. business mgr.
1903
secretary/treasurer
1906-09-

principal investor 1904:
GEN. CHARLES H. TAYLOR

groundskeepers:
? MUDGE 1901
JEROME KELLEY 1903-09-

physician: **T. C. ERB**

FIELD MANAGERS:

JIMMY COLLINS
1901-1906

CHICK STAHL
late 1906

CY YOUNG
1907

GEORGE HUFF
1907

BOB UNGLAUB
1907

JIM
"DEACON"
McGUIRE
1907-1908

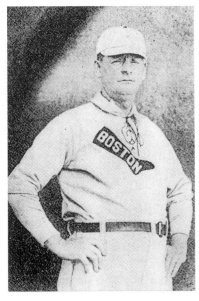

FRED LAKE 1908-1909

BOSTON American League (continued)

PLAYERS:

JOHN "BUCK" FREEMAN
first base, outfield
1901-07

LOUIS CRIGER
catcher 1901-08

JIMMY COLLINS
third baseman 1901-07
(mgr., captain 1901-06)

ALBERT "HOBE" FERRIS
second baseman
1901-07

FRED PARENT
shortstop
1901-07

**DENTON T.
"CY" YOUNG**
pitcher 1901-08
(mgr. 1907)

The 1901 team. BACK ROW (L to R): McKenna, Freeman, Hemphill. NEXT ROW (STANDING): Parent, Cuppy, Young, Kane, Dowd, Stahl. SEATED: Ferris, Criger, Collins (mgr/capt.), Schreckengost, Mitchell. RECLINING: McLean.

BOSTON American League (continued)

CHARLES
HEMPHILL
outfielder
1901

OSSEE SCHRECKENGOST
catcher 1901

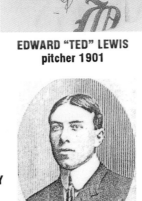

GEORGE CUPPY
pitcher 1901

EDWARD "TED" LEWIS
pitcher 1901

FRED MITCHELL
pitcher 1901-02

1901
ROAD

GEORGE
"SASAFRAS"
WINTER
pitcher
1901-08

TOMMY
DOWD
outfielder
1901

CHARLES
"CHICK"
STAHL
outfielder
1901-06
(mgr. 1906)

1902
HOME

1903
HOME

HARRY GLEASON
infielder 1901-02

THOMAS F. "TULLY" SPARKS
pitcher 1902

"LONG TOM" HUGHES
pitcher 1902-03

PATSY DOUGHERTY
outfielder 1902-04

BOSTON American League (continued)

**GEORGE
"CANDY" LACHANCE**
first baseman
1902-05

BILL DINNEEN
pitcher 1902-07

CHARLES "DUKE" FARRELL
catcher 1903-05

JESSE BURKETT
outfielder
1905

MYRON GRIMSHAW
first baseman
1905-07

**JOHN J.
"JACK" O'BRIEN**
outfielder
1903

NORWOOD GIBSON
pitcher 1903-06

**ALBERT
"KIP" SELBACH**
outfielder
1904-06

BOB UNGLAUB
1st, 3rd baseman
1904-08
(mgr., captain 1907)
(captain 1908)

JOE HARRIS
pitcher 1905-07

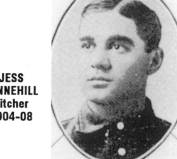

**JESS
TANNEHILL**
pitcher
1904-08

CHARLES ARMBRUSTER
catcher 1905-07

BOSTON American League (continued)

JOHN HOEY
outfielder 1906-08

DANIEL "RALPH" GLAZE
pitcher
1906-08

CHARLES GRAHAM
catcher
1906

CHARLES "HEINIE" WAGNER
shortstop,
second baseman
1906-09-

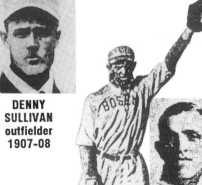

DENNY SULLIVAN
outfielder
1907-08

HARRY R. "CY" MORGAN
pitcher 1907-09

ALFRED "SHODDY" SHAW
catcher 1907

HARRY LORD
third baseman
1907-09-

FRANK OBERLIN
pitcher 1906-07

FRED BURCHELL
pitcher
1907-09

JOHN W. "JACK" KNIGHT
third baseman
1907

"TEX" PRUIETT
pitcher
1907-08

JIMMY BARRETT
outfielder
1907-08

WILLIAM "BUNK" CONGALTON
outfielder 1907

1907 HOME

1908 HOME

BOSTON American League (continued)

CLIFFORD
"GAVVY" CRAVATH
outfielder
1908

FRANK ARRELLANES
pitcher 1908-09-

EDDIE CICOTTE
pitcher 1908-09-

FRANK "POT" LAPORTE
infielder 1908

TRIS SPEAKER
outfielder
1907-09-

HERBERT
"HARRY" NILES
outfielder
1908-09-

AMBROSE McCONNELL
second baseman 1908-09-

JOHN "JACK" THONEY
outfielder 1908-09

HARRY "DOC" GESSLER
outfielder 1908-09
(captain 1909)

ED McFARLAND
catcher 1908

BOSTON American League (continued)

"SMOKY JOE" WOOD
pitcher
1908-09-

The 1908 team—not identified—but Captain Unglaub is in the center of the group, McGuire on his right. Lou Criger is seated on the far right and Eddie Cicotte is reclining on the left.

EDWARD R.
"TUBBY" SPENCER
catcher 1909

GARLAND
"JAKE" STAHL
catcher 1903
first baseman
1908-09-
(captain 1908)

ED KARGER
pitcher
1909

RAY COLLINS
pitcher 1909-

HARRY HOOPER
outfielder 1909-

1909
HOME

CHARLES HALL
pitcher 1909

HARRY WOLTER
pitcher, first baseman
1909

BOSTON National League . . . . NATIONALS, DOVES

OWNERS & OFFICERS:

Principal co-owners 1900-06

ARTHUR H. SODEN
president 1900-06

W. H. CONANT
director 1900-06

J. B. BILLINGS
treasurer 1900-04

WM. "BILLY" ROGERS, sec'y/treas 1902-05

FRANK V. DUNN, owner 1905-06

JOHN HAGGERTY, director

Principal co-owners 1907-09:

GEORGE B. DOVEY
president

JOHN DOVEY
secretary
bus. mgr.

J. P. HARRIS, director
groundskeeper: TOM PALLAS
grounds supt.: JOHN HAGGERTY
chief usher: GENE FOSTER

trainers:

BILLY EDWARDS

JIM NEARY

FIELD MANAGERS:

FRANK SELEE
1900-1901

ALBERT C. BUCKENBERGER
1902-1904

FRED TENNEY
1905-1907

1900 HOME

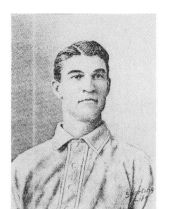

JOE KELLEY
1908

FRANK BOWERMAN
1909

HARRY SMITH
late 1909

BOSTON National League (continued)

PLAYERS:

The 1900 team. TOP ROW (L to R): Lowe, Barry, Stahl, Duffy, Clarke. MIDDLE ROW: Cuppy, Freeman, Sullivan, Dinneen, Willis, Lewis. SEATED: Clements, Hamilton, Nichols, Selee (mgr.), Long, Tenney, Collins.

BILLY SULLIVAN
catcher 1900

BILLY HAMILTON
outfielder 1900-01

JOHN C. "SHAD" BARRY
utility 1900-01

CHARLES "CHICK" STAHL
outfielder 1900

FRED TENNEY
fiirst baseman 1900-07
(manager 1905-07)
(captain 1903-07)

JIMMY COLLINS
third baseman 1900

**EDWARD M.
"TED" LEWIS**
pitcher 1900

CHARLES A. "KID" NICHOLS
pitcher 1900-01

HUGH DUFFY
outfielder 1900
(captain 1900)

BOSTON National League (continued)

JOHN F. "BUCK" FREEMAN
outfield, first base
1900

HERMAN LONG
shortstop 1900-02

BOBBY LOWE
second baseman
1900-01

DICK COOLEY
outfield, first base
1901-04

MALACHI KITTRIDGE
catcher 1901-03

PAT MORAN
catcher 1901-05

LORENZO "ED" GREMINGER
third baseman 1902-03

WILLIAM "BOILERYARD" CLARKE
catcher
1900

VIC WILLIS
pitcher 1900-05

JIMMY SLAGLE
outfielder
1901

FRED CROLIUS
outfielder 1901

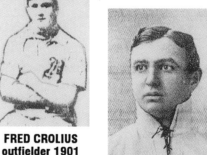

PATRICK J. "DOC" CARNEY
outfielder, pitcher
1901-04

BILL DINNEEN
pitcher 1900-01

CHARLES R. "TOGIE" PITTINGER
pitcher 1900-04

EUGENE DEMONTREVILLE
second, third base
1901-02

ROBERT LAWSON
pitcher 1901

BILLY LUSH
outfielder 1901-02

1901 HOME

1902 HOME

BOSTON National League (continued)

JOHN MALARKEY
pitcher 1902-03

CHARLES DEXTER
utility 1902-03

JOSEPH B. STANLEY
outfielder 1903-04

FRANK BONNER
second baseman 1903

ED McNICHOL
pitcher 1904

PHIL GEIER
outfielder 1904

TOM NEEDHAM
catcher 1904-07

BILL LAUTERBORN
second baseman 1904-05

MAL EASON
pitcher 1902

ERNIE COURTNEY
utility 1902

IRVIN K. "KAISER" WILHELM
pitcher 1904-05

WILEY PIATT
pitcher 1903

JIM DELAHANTY
utility 1904-05

ED ABBATICCHIO
infielder 1903-05

FRED RAYMER
second baseman 1904-05

TOM FISHER
pitcher 1904

GEORGE BARCLAY
outfielder 1904-05

VIRGIN W. "RIP" CANNELL
outfielder 1904-05

BOSTON National League (continued)

IRVING M. "YOUNG CY" YOUNG
pitcher 1905-08

HARRY WOLVERTON
third baseman 1905

PATRICK H.
"COZY" DOLAN
outfielder
1905-06

CHARLES C.
"CHICK" FRASER
pitcher 1905

JOHN J.
"JACK" O'NEIL
catcher 1906

CLARENCE H.
"GINGER" BEAUMONT
outfielder 1907-09

GEORGE BROWNE
outfielder 1908

DAN McGANN
first baseman
1908

DAVE BRAIN
third baseman
1906-07

GEORGE E.
"DEL" HOWARD
utility 1906-07

CLAUDE RITCHEY
second baseman
1907-09

1908
HOME

1908
ROAD

SAMUEL W.
BROWN
catcher
1906-07

ALLIE STROBEL
second baseman
1905-06

AL BRIDWELL
shortstop
1906-07

PATSY FLAHERTY
pitcher 1907-08

GUS DORNER
pitcher 1906-09

BILL SWEENEY
infielder 1907-09-

JACK HANNIFIN
third baseman
1908

EUGENE J. GOOD
outfielder 1906

1907
HOME

1907
ROAD

JOHNNY BATES
outfielder 1906-09

VIVAN A.
"VIVE" LINDAMAN
pitcher 1906-09

FRANCIS X.
"BIG JEFF" PFEFFER
pitcher 1906-08

JAKE BOULTES
pitcher 1907-09

JOE KELLEY
outfielder 1908
(mgr., captain 1908)

BOSTON National League (continued)

BILL DAHLEN
shortstop 1908-09-

FRANK BOWERMAN
catcher 1908-09
(mgr. 1909) (capt. 1905)

**GEORGE
"PEACHES" GRAHAM**
catcher 1908-09-

ALONZO "AL" MATTERN
pitcher 1908-09

ROY THOMAS
outfielder 1909

LEW RICHIE
pitcher 1909

OLIVER "KIRBY" WHITE
pitcher 1909

**1909
ROAD**

DAVID "BEALS" BECKER
outfielder 1908-09

HARRY SMITH
catcher 1908-09
(mgr. late 1909)

CECIL FERGUSON
pitcher 1908-09-

CHARLES STARR
second baseman 1909

**ALFRED
"SHODDY" SHAW**
catcher 1909

FRED BECK
first base, outfield
1909

**WM. A.
"CHICK" AUTRY**
first baseman
1909

BROOKLYN National League .... SUPERBAS, TROLLEY DODGERS

OWNERS & OFFICERS:

CHARLES H. EBBETS, Sr.
co-owner, president
1900-1909-

HARRY VON DER HORST
co-owner, secretary
1900-1904

**FREDERICK A.
"GUS" ABELL**
co-owner
VP/treasurer
1900-1907

directors:

EDW. "NED" HANLON

GEO. H. WATSON
WM. G. BYRNE
A. S. WALL
TOMMY SIMPSON
CHAS. EBBETS Jr.

HENRY W. MEDICUS
treasurer 1905-

GEORGE H. WATSON
secretary 1904-

vice president (1907): ROBERT A. WRIGHT

groundskeeper: ? PARKER

trainer: ? COMERFORD

FIELD MANAGERS:

EDWARD H. "NED" HANLON
1900-1905

PATSY DONOVAN
1906-1908

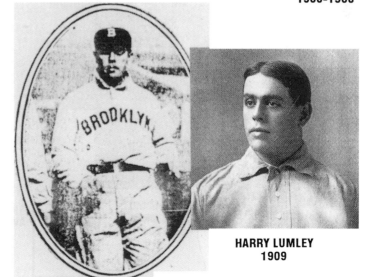

HARRY LUMLEY
1909

BROOKLYN National League (continued)

PATRICK H. "COZY" DOLAN
outfielder 1901-02

CHARLES IRWIN
shortstop, third base
1901-02

VIRGIL GARVIN
pitcher 1902-04

JOHN J. "JACK" DOYLE
first baseman 1903-04
(captain 1903)

HENRY SCHMIDT
pitcher 1903

FRED JACKLITSCH
catcher 1903-04

TIM FLOOD
second base, outfield
1902-03

LEROY EVANS
pitcher 1902-03

ED HOUSEHOLDER
outfielder 1903

ED WHEELER
utility infield
1902

LOU RITTER
catcher 1902-08

JOHN DOBBS
outfielder 1903-05

SAMMY STRANG (NICKLIN)
third baseman 1903-04

The 1903 team. STANDING (L to R): O. Jordan, Strang, McCreedie, Dahlen, Thielman, Vickers, Doyle, Jacklitsch, (?), McManus. MIDDLE ROW: Householder, Evans, Flood, Schmidt, Sheckard. BOTTOM ROW: Jones, Hearne, Broderick, Gabriel, Ritter.

BILL REIDY
pitcher, utility 1903-04

JACK DOSCHER
pitcher 1903-06

**MICHAEL J.
"DUDE" McCORMICK**
third baseman 1904

BILL BERGEN, catcher 1904-09-

ED POOLE, pitcher 1904

HARRY LUMLEY
outfielder
1904-09-
(manager 1909)
(captain 1908-)

OSCAR JONES
pitcher 1903-05

**HARRY H.
"DOC" GESSLER**
outfield,
first base
1903-06

CHARLES BABB
shortstop 1904-05

FRANK "POP" DILLON
first baseman 1904

JOHN J. "JACK" CRONIN
pitcher 1904

EMIL "HEINIE" BATCH
third base, outfield
1904-07

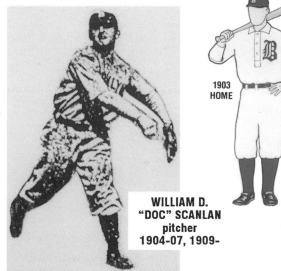

**WILLIAM D.
"DOC" SCANLAN**
pitcher
1904-07, 1909-

1903
HOME

1905
HOME

BROOKLYN National League (continued)

BOB HALL
utility
1905

THOMAS L. "RED" OWENS
second base 1905

CHARLES F. MALAY
second base, outfield
1905

**MAL
EASON**
pitcher
1905-06

PHIL LEWIS
shortstop 1905-08

JAMES P. "DOC" CASEY
third baseman 1906-07
(captain 1906-07)

**CHARLES
"WHITEY"
ALPERMAN**
second baseman
1906-09

TIM JORDAN
first baseman 1906-09-

ELMER STRICKLETT
pitcher 1905-07

JOHN HUMMEL
utility 1905-09

JOHN R. "HARRY" McINTYRE
pitcher 1905-09

JOHN A. "JACK" McCARTHY
outfielder 1906-07

JIM PASTORIUS
pitcher 1906-09

WILLIAM "BILLY" MALONEY
outfielder
1906-08

BROOKLYN National League (continued)

The 1906 team. STANDING (L to R): McCarthy, Lumley, Maloney, Hummel, (?), Bergen, Lewis, McIntyre.
MIDDLE ROW: Jordan, Casey, Donovan, Pastorius, Eason. BOTTOM: Butler, Stricklett, Batch, Alperman.

GEORGE N. "NAP" RUCKER
pitcher
1907-09-

GEORGE BELL
pitcher 1907-09-

AL BURCH
outfielder
1907-09-

1907
ROAD

TOMMY SHEEHAN
third baseman 1908

HARRY PATTEE
second baseman
1908

JOE DUNN
catcher
1908-09

TOMMY McMILLIAN
shortstop
1908-09

**IRVIN K.
"KAISER" WILHELM**
pitcher 1908-09-

JIMMY SEBRING
outfielder 1909

**JAMES E.
"EGGIE" LENNOX**
third baseman
1909-

ZACH WHEAT
outfielder
1909-

WILLIAM "DOC" MARSHALL
catcher 1909

**WALLY
CLEMENT**
outfielder
1909

**1909
HOME**

**1909
ROAD**

**ALEXANDER
"RED" DOWNEY**
outfielder
1909

JOE KUSTUS
outfielder
1909

GEORGE HUNTER
pitcher, outfield
1909-

**PRYOR M.
"HUMPY" McELVEEN**
third baseman 1909-

CHICAGO American League . . . . WHITE STOCKINGS, WHITE SOX

OWNERS & OFFICERS:

CHARLES A. COMISKEY
owner, president

secretary/treas.: **GEORGE HEANEY**

**CHARLES
FREDERICKS**
sec'y/treas.
1905

directors:
 **JAMES CALLAHAN
 CLARK GRIFFITH
 GEORGE HEANEY
 WM. LACHEMEIER
 CHAS. FREDERICKS
 TONY MULLANE
 G. SIMMONS**

trainer:
 **? CONIBEAR
 JIM BARDELL**

FIELD MANAGERS:

CLARK GRIFFITH
1901-1902

JIMMY CALLAHAN
1903-1904

**1901
HOME**

BILLY SULLIVAN
1909

FIELDER JONES
mid 1904-1908

CHICAGO American League (continued)

THE PLAYERS:

CLARK GRIFFITH
pitcher 1901-02
(mgr., captain 1901-02)

**WILLIAM E.
"DUMMY" HOY**
outfielder
1901

FRED HARTMAN
third baseman 1901

WILLIAM "FRANK" SHUGART
shortstop 1901

JOE SUGDEN
catcher
1901

JOHN KATOLL
pitcher 1901-02

FIELDER JONES
outfielder 1901-08
(mgr. 1904-08)
(captain 1905-08)

FRANK ISBELL
first baseman, utility
1901-09

SAMUEL "SANDOW" MERTES
second baseman, utility
1901-02

**JIMMY
CALLAHAN**
pitcher, utility
1901-05
(mgr. 1903-04)
(captain 1904)

**1901
ROAD**

JIMMY BURKE
third baseman
1901

JOHN SKOPEC
pitcher 1901

CHICAGO American League (continued)

**WILLIAM J.
"BILLY" SULLIVAN**
catcher 1901-09
(mgr. 1909)
(captain 1903)

HERMAS "HERM" McFARLAND
outfielder 1901-02

ROY PATTERSON, pitcher 1901-07

THOMAS "TIDO" DALY
second baseman 1902-03

VIRGIL GARVIN
pitcher 1902

WILEY PIATT
pitcher 1901-02

**ERVIN K.
HARVEY**
pitcher,
outfielder
1901

SAMMY STRANG (NICKLIN)
third baseman 1902

The 1902 team. STANDING (L to R): E. McFarland, H. McFarland, Piat, Patterson, Fredericks (sec'y.), Daly, Jones, Robertson. MIDDLE ROW: Garvin, Isbell, Griffith (mgr.). BOTTOM: Davis, Green, Sullivan, Callahan.

CHICAGO American League (continued)

GEORGE DAVIS
shortstop, infield utility
1902, 1904-09

EDWARD W. McFARLAND
catcher 1902-07

EDWARD "DAVEY" DUNKLE
pitcher 1903

GEORGE "MAGGIE" MAGOON
second base
1903

WILLIAM "DUCKY" HOLMES
outfielder 1903-05

PATRICK FLAHERTY
pitcher 1903-04

1903
HOME

1904
ROAD

EDWARD "DANNY" GREEN
outfielder 1902-05

LEE TANNEHILL
shortstop, third base
1903-09-

NICK ALTROCK
pitcher 1903-09

FRANK "YIP" OWEN
pitcher 1903-09

WILLIAM H. HALLMAN
outfielder 1903

CHICAGO American League (continued)

G. HARRIS "DOC" WHITE
pitcher 1903-09-

The 1904 team. STANDING (L to R): L. Tannehill, Green, Welch, Isbell, Sullivan, G. Davis, E. McFarland, Donahue. KNEELING: Dundon, Altrock, Jones (mgr.), White, Owens, Holmes.

FRANK SMITH
pitcher 1904-09-

JOHN "JIGGS" DONAHUE
first baseman 1904-09

AUGUSTUS "GUS" DUNDON
second baseman 1904-06

1905
HOME

ED WALSH
pitcher 1904-09-

CHICAGO American League (continued)

CLIFFORD "GAVVY" CRAVATH
outfielder 1909

FRED PAYNE
catcher 1909-

HARRY SUTER
pitcher 1909

BILL BURNS
pitcher 1909-

BARNEY REILLY
second baseman 1909

**CHARLES W. "BOBBY"
MESSENGER**
outfielder 1909-

DAVE ALTIZER
utility infielder 1909

WILLIS COLE
outfielder 1909

ROLAND "CUKE" BARROWS
outfielder 1909

1906
HOME

1908
ROAD

1909
HOME

CHICAGO National League .... REMNANTS, COLTS, ORPHANS, CUBS

OWNERS & OFFICERS:

JAMES A. HART
owner, president
1900-1905

CHARLES W. MURPHY
owner,
president
1905-09-

CHARLES WILLIAMS
sec'y/treas.

secretary: ? THOMAS

directors:
JOHN R. WALSH
FRANK CHANCE
CHARLES P. TAFT

groundskeeper: CHARLES KUHN

trainers:
JACK McCORMICK
A. BERT SEMMENS

FIELD MANAGERS:

TOM LOFTUS
1900-1901

FRANK SELEE
1902-1905

FRANK CHANCE
mid 1905-1909-

The 1902 team. STANDING (L to R): Taylor, Chance, O'Hagen, Selee (mgr.), W. Williams, Miller, Tinker. MIDDLE: St. Vrain, Slagle, Kling, A. Williams, Gardner, Lowe. BOTTOM: Jones, Congalton, Schaefer, Menefee, Dexter, Rhoades.

CHICAGO National League (continued)

THE PLAYERS:

VIRGIL GARVIN
pitcher 1900

JIMMY CALLAHAN
pitcher 1900

CLARK GRIFFITH
pitcher 1900

TIM DONAHUE
catcher 1900

JIMMY RYAN
outfielder 1900
(captain 1900)

BILLY CLINGMAN
shortstop 1900

CLARENCE "CUPID" CHILDS
second baseman 1900-01

**PATRICK H.
"COZY" DOLAN**
outfielder
1900-01

**SAMUEL B.
"SANDOW" MERTES**
first baseman,
outfielder
1900

BILL EVERETT
first baseman 1900

BILL BRADLEY
first, third baseman
1900

**SAMMY STRANG
(NICKLIN)**
third baseman
1900

MAL EASON
pitcher 1900-02

EDWARD "DANNY" GREEN
outfielder 1900-01

**WILLIAM J.
"BARRY" McCORMICK**
shortstop, third base
1900-01

**"LONG TOM"
HUGHES**
pitcher
1900-01

CHARLES DEXTER
utility
1900-02

CHICAGO National League (continued)

JOHN "JOCKO" MENEFEE
pitcher 1900-03

**JOHN A.
"JACK" McCARTHY**
outfielder
1900, 1903-05

**JOHN W.
"JACK" TAYLOR**
pitcher, utility
1900-03,
1906-07

JOHN GANZELL
first baseman
1900

FRANK CHANCE
catcher, outfielder, first baseman
1900-09-
(mgr. 1905-09-)
(captain 1904-09)

JOHNNY KLING
catcher 1900-09-

1902
ROAD

CHICAGO National League (continued)

**TULLY F.
"TOPSY" HARTSEL**
outfielder 1901

**JOHN J.
"JACK" DOYLE**
first baseman 1901
(captain 1901)

**HERMAN
"GERMANY" SCHAEFER**
utility 1901-02

**ARTHUR F.
"BILL" WILLIAMS**
utility 1902

**WALTER M.
"POP" WILLIAMS**
pitcher 1902-03

BOBBY LOWE
second baseman
1902-03
(captain 1903)

CARL LUNDGREN
pitcher 1902-09

FRED RAYMER
shortstop, third base
1901

GEORGE E. "RUBE" WADDELL
pitcher 1901

HARRY O'HAGEN
first baseman
1902

JAMES ST. VRAIN
pitcher 1902

MIKE KAHOE
catcher, utility
1901-02, 1907

**DAKIN E.
MILLER**
outfielder
1902

**WILLIAM
"BUNK" CONGALTON**
outfielder
1902

JOHN DOBBS
outfielder
1902-03

DAVY JONES
outfielder 1902-04

JIMMY SLAGLE
outfielder
1902-08

CHICAGO National League (continued)

1903
HOME

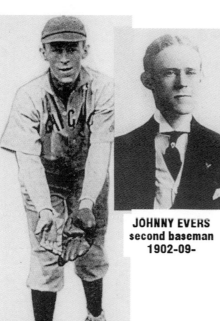

JOHNNY EVERS
second baseman
1902-09-

OTTO WILLIAMS
utility
1903-04

JAMES P. "DOC" CASEY
third baseman 1903-05

JOE TINKER
shortstop 1902-09-

DICK HARLEY
outfielder
1903

The 1903 team. STANDING (L to R): Tinker, Taylor, Lundgren, Harley, Evers, Kling, Weimer. MIDDLE: Lowe, (?), Chance, Selee (mgr.), Menefee, Jones, Wicker. RECLINING: Slagle, Casey.

BOB WICKER
pitcher 1903-06

JAKE WEIMER
pitcher 1903-05

MORDECAI P.C. "THREE-FINGER" BROWN
pitcher 1904-09-

BILLY MALONEY
outfielder
1905

**HERBERT
"BUTTONS" BRIGGS**
pitcher 1904-05

**FRANCIS X.
"BIG JEFF" PFEFFER**
pitcher 1905

JOHN C. "SHAD" BARRY
first base, outfield
1904-05

ARTHUR F. "CIRCUS SOLLY" HOFMAN
utility 1904-09-

**FRANK
"WILDFIRE" SCHULTE**
outfielder
1904-09-

FRANK CORRIDON
pitcher 1904

ED REULBACH
pitcher 1905-09-

SAMUEL J.T.
"JIMMY" SHECKARD
outfielder 1906-09-

PAT MORAN
catcher 1906-09

JOHN A. "JACK" PFIESTER
pitcher 1906-09-

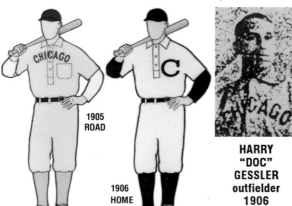

1905
ROAD

1906
HOME

HARRY
"DOC"
GESSLER
outfielder
1906

The 1906 team (116 wins). STANDING (L to R): Brown, Pfiester, Hofman, C. Williams (sec'y.), Overall, Reulbach, Kling. MIDDLE: Gessler, Taylor, Steinfeldt, McCormick, Chance (mgr.), Sheckard, Moran, Schulte. BOTTOM: Lundgren, Walsh, Evers, Slagle, Tinker.

ORVAL OVERALL
pitcher 1906-09-

CHARLES
"CHICK"
FRASER
pitcher
1907-09

BLAINE A.
"KID" DURBIN
pitcher, outfielder
1907-08

HENRY "HEINIE"
ZIMMERMAN
second base,
infield utility
1907-09-

GEORGE E.
"DEL" HOWARD
first base, outfielder
1907-09

JOHNNY KANE
first base, outfield
1909-

JIMMY ARCHER
catcher 1909-

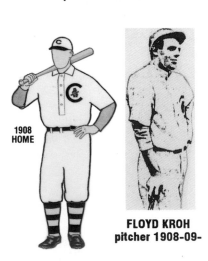

1908
HOME

FLOYD KROH
pitcher 1908-09-

HARRY
STEINFELDT
third baseman
1906-09-

ZERIAH "RIP" HAGERMAN
pitcher 1909

IRV
HIGGINBOTHAM
pitcher
1909

1909
ROAD

CINCINNATI National League . . . . REDS

OWNERS & OFFICERS:

JOHN T. BRUSH
owner 1900-02

AUGUST "GARRY" HERRMANN
president 1900-09
co-owner 1902-09

FRANK BANCROFT
business manager
1900-09

N. ASHLEY LLOYD
sec'y/treas.
1900-02

JOHN D. ELLISON
director

MAX FLEISHMAN
sec'y/treas.
1902-08

JULIUS FLEISHMAN
sec'y 1903

GEO. B. COX
director

executive secretary 1903: **MARY SULLIVAN**
asst. business mgr. 1906: **GEORGE SCHOETTLE**

directors:
THOMAS J. LOGAN
W. J. ODELL
W. H. O'BRIEN
JOHN C. GALLAGHER

trainers:
ED MACKALL
CHRIS CLINE
groundskeepers:
JOHN SCHWAB
MATTY SCHWAB

scouts:
TED SULLIVAN
LOUIS HEILBRONER
TOM McCARTHY

FIELD MANAGERS:

BOB ALLEN
1900

JOHN "BID" McPHEE
1901-1902

FRANK BANCROFT
mid 1902

JOE KELLEY
late 1902-1905

NED HANLON
1906-1907

JOHN GANZELL
1908

CLARK GRIFFITH
1909

CINCINNATI National League (continued)

WILLIAM E. "DUMMY" HOY
outfielder 1902

ERWIN BECK
utility
1902

ED POOLE
pitcher 1902-03

HENRY THIELMAN
pitcher 1902

MIKE DONLIN
outfielder 1902-04

CLARENCE CURRIE
pitcher 1902

JOE KELLEY
utility
1902-06
(mgr. 1902-05)
(captain 1903-04)

The 1903 team. TOP ROW (L to R): Allemang, Magoon, Morrisey, Wood, Hahn. MIDDLE: Harper, Bergen, Steinfeldt, Peer, Wiggs, Corcoran, Ewing, Hooker. BOTTOM: Peitz, Sutthoff, Donlin, Kelley (mgr.), Seymour, Beckley, Poole, Phillips.

GEORGE L. "BOB" EWING
pitcher
1902-09

THOMAS P. DALY
second base 1903

PATRICK H. "COZY" DOLAN
first baseman,
outfielder
1903-05

CHARLES W. "JACK" HARPER
pitcher 1903-06

CINCINNATI National League (continued)

1905
HOME

ORVILLE WOODRUFF
second, third baseman
1904

CLAUDE ELLIOTT
pitcher 1904

FRED "FRITZ" ODWELL
outfielder 1904-07

**CHARLES
"GABBY" STREET**
catcher 1904-05

WIN KELLUM
pitcher 1904

MILLER HUGGINS
second baseman 1904-09

**GEORGE
"ADMIRAL" SCHLEI**
catcher
1904-08

The 1905 team. TOP ROW (L to R): Dolan, Chech, Ewing, Phelps, Overall, Harper, Odwell. MIDDLE: Sebring, Huggins, Street, Seymour, Kelley (mgr.), Blankenship, Corcoran, Walker, Steinfeldt. BOTTOM: Schlei, Bridwell, Hahn.

CINCINNATI National League (continued)

JIMMY SEBRING
outfielder 1904-05

TOM WALKER
pitcher 1904-05

JOHN SIEGLE
outfielder
1905-06

JOHN C. "SHAD" BARRY
utility 1905-06

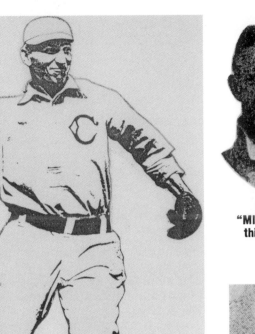

HANS LOBERT
shortstop, third base
1905-09-
(captain 1909)

AL BRIDWELL
third base, outfield 1905

ORVAL OVERALL
pitcher 1905-06

CHARLES CHECH
pitcher 1905-06

ED PHELPS
catcher 1905-06

**HOMER
SMOOT**
outfield
1906

FRANK JUDE
outfielder 1906

JIM DELAHANTY
infielder 1906

**HARRY H.
"MIKE" MOWREY**
third baseman
1905-09

**PATRICK
"PADDY"
LIVINGSTON**
catcher 1906

CARL DRUHOT
pitcher 1906

CINCINNATI National League (continued)

BOB WICKER
pitcher 1906

CHICK FRASER
pitcher 1906

CHARLES HALL
pitcher 1906-07

DEL MASON
pitcher 1906-07

ART KRUGER
outfielder 1907

JOHN GANZELL
first baseman 1907-08
(mgr. 1908)
(captain 1907-08)

JOHN "SNAKE" DEAL
first baseman
1906

JAKE WEIMER
pitcher 1906-08

JOHN B. "LARRY" McLEAN
catcher 1906-09-

1906 HOME

ROY HITT
pitcher 1907

FRED SMITH
pitcher
1907

1907 ROAD

JOHNNY KANE
utility 1907-08

MIKE MITCHELL
outfielder 1907-09-

ALFONSO "LEFTY" DAVIS
outfielder 1907

CINCINNATI National League (continued)

ANDY COAKLEY
pitcher 1907-08

BILL CAMPBELL
pitcher 1907-09

DICK HOBLITZELL
first baseman 1908-09-

JEAN DUBUC
pitcher 1908-09

**GEORGE H.
"DODE" PASKERT**
outfielder
1907-09-

BOB SPADE
pitcher 1907-09-

RUDY HULSWITT
shortstop 1908

JOHN A. "JACK" ROWAN
pitcher 1908-09-

BOB BESCHER
outfielder 1908-09-

The 1908 team. TOP ROW (L to R): Weimer, Mowrey, Spade, Ewing, Ganzell (mgr.), McLean, Mitchell, Lobert, Tozer, McCarthy. MIDDLE: Schlei, Coakley, Campbell, Pearce. BOTTOM: Daley, Kane, Huggins, McGilvray, Upp, Hulswitt, Paskert.

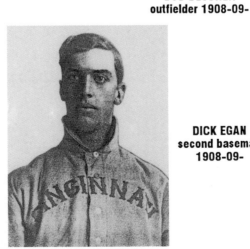

DICK EGAN
second baseman
1908-09-

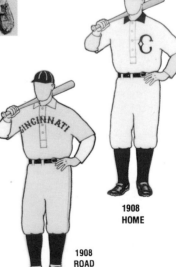

1908
HOME

1908
ROAD

CINCINNATI National League (continued)

ENNIS T. "REBEL" OAKES
outfielder 1909

TOM DOWNEY
shortstop 1909–

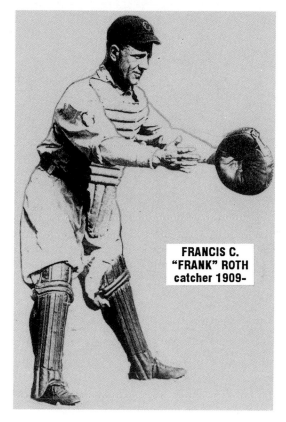

**FRANCIS C.
"FRANK" ROTH**
catcher 1909–

1909
ROAD

ART FROMME
pitcher 1909–

HARRY GASPAR
pitcher 1909–

WARD MILLER
outfielder
1909–

CLEVELAND American League . . . . .BLUES, BRONCHOS, NAPS

OWNERS & OFFICERS:

JOHN F. KILFOYLE
owner, president
1901-1908

directors:
CHARLES HIGBY
J. A. FORESTNEY
G. E. FREY

secretary:
JOSEPH McKEON 1901
? CHAPMAN 1902

CHARLES W. SOMERS
vice president 1908
president 1909

ERNEST S. BARNARD
secretary
vice pres.
1903-09-

physician: Dr. CASTLE

groundskeepers:
HANK HAMILTON 1903
WILLIAM VAUGHAN 1904
CHARLES MADDOCKS 1904

trainer: **DOC PAYNE**

FIELD MANAGERS:

JAMES McALEER
1901

BILL ARMOUR
1902-1904

"DEACON" JIM McGUIRE
late 1909-

**NAPOLEON
"NAP", "LARRY"
LAJOIE**
1905-late 1909

THE PLAYERS:

CLEVELAND American League (continued)

BILL BRADLEY
third baseman 1901-09-

DANNY SHAY
shortstop
1901

FRANK SCHEIBECK
shortstop 1901

EDWARD P. SCOTT
pitcher 1901

HENRY P. "PETE" DOWLING
pitcher 1901

EARL MOORE
pitcher 1901-07

GEORGE "CANDY" LACHANCE
first baseman 1901

JOHN J. "JACK" O'BRIEN
outfielder 1901

ERVIN K. HARVEY
pitcher, outfielder
1901-02

1901 HOME

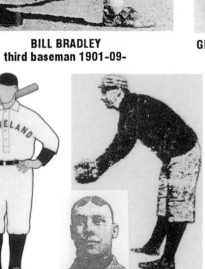

ERWIN BECK
utility 1901

BILL HOFFER
pitcher 1901

WILLIAM F. HART
pitcher 1901

BOB WOOD
catcher
1901-02

OLLIE PICKERING
outfielder 1901-02

**JOHN "JACK"
McCARTHY**
outfielder
1901-03

CLEVELAND American League (continued)

OSCAR STREIT
pitcher 1902

CHARLES HICKMAN
utility 1902-04, 08

FRANK BONNER
second baseman
1902
(captain 1902)

JOHN "JACK" THONEY
utility 1902-03

JOHN GOCHNAUER
shortstop 1902-03

CLARENCE WRIGHT
pitcher 1902-03

1902
HOME

NAPOLEON LAJOIE
second baseman 1902-09-
(mgr. 1905-09)
(captain 1902-09)

1902
ROAD

The 1902 team. STANDING (L to R): Bernhard, Moore, Hickman, Joss, Bradley, Hess. MIDDLE: Bemis, Bay, Pickering, Armour (mgr.), McCarthy, Gochnaur. BOTTOM: Flick, Thoney, Lajoie, Wood.

CLEVELAND American League (continued)

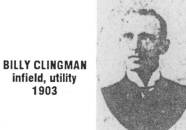

ADRIAN "ADDIE" JOSS
pitcher 1902-09-

OTTO HESS
pitcher 1902, 1904-08

ELMER FLICK
outfielder 1902-09-

HARRY BAY
outfielder 1902-08

BILL BERNHARD
pitcher 1902-07

HARRY BEMIS
catcher 1902-09-

BILLY CLINGMAN
infield, utility
1903

FRANCIS "RED", "FRANK"
DONAHUE
pitcher 1903-05

CLEVELAND American League (continued)

FRED ABBOTT
catcher 1903-04

BILLY LUSH
outfielder 1904

WILLIAM SCHWARTZ
first baseman
1904

1904
ROAD

CLAUDE ROSSMAN
first baseman 1904, 1906

TERRY TURNER
shortstop, utility 1904-09-

ERNEST
"RUBE" VINSON
outfielder
1904-05

ROBERT "DUSTY" RHOADES
pitcher 1903-09

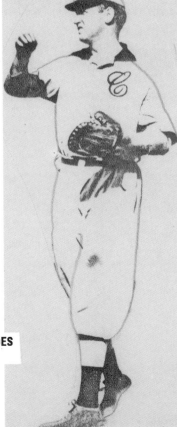

CHARLEY CARR
first baseman 1904-05

The 1904 team. TOP ROW (L to R): Moore, Rossman, Donahue, Hess, Curtiss, Pastor, Schwartz, Hickey, Rhoades. MIDDLE: Bernhard, Abbott, Lajoie, Armour (mgr.), Joss, Hickman, Flick. BOTTOM: Bay, Bemis, O'Hara, Turner, Bradley.

FRED "FRITZ" BUELOW
catcher 1904-06

JIM JACKSON
outfielder 1905-06

WM. "BUNK" CONGALTON
outfielder 1905-07

HOWARD WAKEFIELD
catcher 1905, 1907

**GEORGE
"FIREBRAND" STOVALL**
first baseman 1904-09-

**WILLIAM
"JAP" BARBEAU**
third baseman
1905-06

GLENN LIEBHARDT
pitcher 1906-09

**NICHOLAS
KAHL**
second baseman
1905

JAY "NIG" CLARKE
catcher 1905-09-

DETROIT American League . . . . TIGERS

OWNERS & OFFICERS:

JAMES BURNS
co-owner, president
1900-01

GEORGE STALLINGS
co-owner
1900-01

SAM ANGUS
owner, president
1902-04

BILL YAWKEY
co-owner 1904-07
V.P. 1903-04
president 1904-07

FRANK NAVIN
co-owner 1904-07
sec'y./treas./bus. mgr. 1904-07
owner, president 1908-09-

1901
HOME

**FRANK
DWYER**
bus. mgr.
1901-03

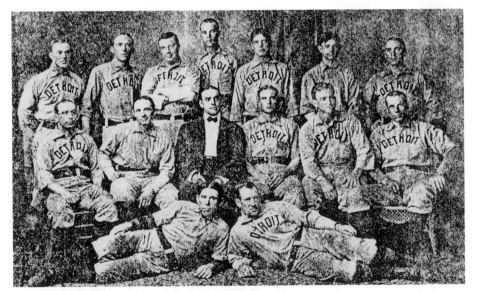

WM. MAY
business mgr.
1902

directors 1901:
GEORGE BURNHAM
JOHN FITZPATRICK
? McALLISTER

officers 1902:
secretary: FRANK COOK
treasurer: EDW. H. DOYLE
attorney: JAMES McNAMARA

sec'y/treas. 1903:
A. C. "LEE" HENRY

sec'y/treas. 1905:
CHARLES SCHUMM

attorney:
THOMAS J. NAVIN

groundskeeper: BILL CLINE
KLEIN

ticket mgr.: PHILO ROBINSON

trainers:
ANDY RUDOLPH
HARRY TUTHILL
ALLIE DAY

The 1901 team. TOP ROW (L to R): Shaw, Miller, Cronin, Elberfield, Owens, Yeager, Barrett. MIDDLE: Casey, Holmes, Stallings (mgr.), Siever, McAllister, Dillon. RECLINING: Nance, Gleason.

DETROIT American League (continued)

FIELD MANAGERS:

GEORGE STALLINGS
1901

FRANK DWYER
1902

ED BARROW
1903-Aug. 1904

BOBBY LOWE
Aug.-Sept. 1904
(captain 1904)

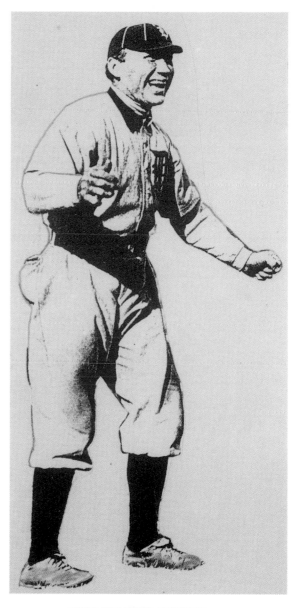

HUGH "EE-YAH" JENNINGS
1907-1909-

The 1902 team. STANDING (L to R): Miller, Mullin, McAllister, Dillon, Siever, McGuire, Cronin. MIDDLE: Harley, Yeager, May (bus. mgr.), Dwyer (mgr.), Mercer, Holmes, Elberfield. BOTTOM: Buelow, Gleason, Casey, Barrett.

BILL ARMOUR
1905-1906

DETROIT American League (continued)

THE PLAYERS:

FRANK "POP" DILLON
first baseman 1901-02

WILLIAM J. "KID" GLEASON
second baseman 1901-02

ALFRED "SHODDY" SHAW
catcher 1901

WILLIAM G. "KID" NANCE
outfielder 1901

1902
ROAD

JAMES P. "DOC" CASEY
third baseman 1901-02
(captain 1901-02)

JAMES "JIMMY" BARRETT
outfielder 1901-05
(captain 1905)

EMIL FRISK
pitcher 1901

JAMES W. "DUCKY" HOLMES
outfielder 1901-02
(captain 1902)

**ROSCOE
"ROXY", "RUBBERLEGS"
MILLER**
pitcher 1901-02

NORMAN "KID" ELBERFIELD
shortstop 1901-03

JOE YEAGER
pitcher, utility 1901-03

**LEWIS W. "SPORT"
McALLISTER**
catcher, utility
1901-03

DETROIT American League (continued)

JOHN "JACK" CRONIN
pitcher 1901-02

Ed SIEVER
pitcher 1901-02,
1907-08

The 1903 team. TOP ROW (L to R): McGuire, McAllister, Kitson, Elberfield, Buelow, Donovan. MIDDLE: Carr, Barrow (mgr.), Eason, Crawford, Yeager, Deering, Mullin. BOTTOM: Barrett, Smith, Gessler, Jones, Lush, Kissinger.

ERWIN BECK
utility 1902

FRED W. "FRITZ" BUELOW
catcher 1901-04

**ALOYSIUS
"WISH" EGAN**
pitcher 1902

**GEORGE
"WIN" MERCER**
pitcher
1902

DICK HARLEY
outfielder 1902

CHARLES "RUBE" KISINGER
pitcher 1902-03

1903
ROAD

JACK O'CONNOR
catcher 1903

ALFONSO "LEFTY" DAVIS
outfielder 1903

JESS TANNEHILL
pitcher 1903

WILLIAM "WID" CONROY
utility 1903-08

HENRY "MONTE" BEVILLE
catcher 1903-04

DAVE FULTZ
outfielder
1903-05

WILLIAM "WILLIE" KEELER
outfielder 1903-09
(captain 1909)

ERNIE COURTNEY
shortstop 1903

WILLIAM WOLFE
pitcher 1903-04

HARRY HOWELL
pitcher 1903

NORMAN "KID" ELBERFIELD
shortstop 1903-09
(mgr. late 1908)
(captain 1908)

JOHN DEERING
pitcher 1903

AMBROSE PUTTMANN
pitcher 1903-05

NEW YORK American League (continued)

JACK CHESBRO
pitcher 1903-09

"LONG TOM" HUGHES
pitcher 1904

JOHN "JACK" THONEY
utility 1904

JIM "DEACON" McGUIRE
catcher 1904-07

JOHN P. "JACK", "RED" KLEINOW
catcher 1904-09-

AL ORTH
pitcher 1904-09

PATSY DOUGHERTY
outfielder 1904-06

JOHN ANDERSON
utility 1904-05

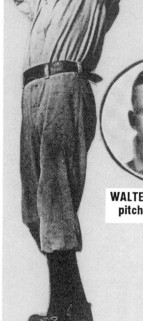

WALTER CLARKSON
pitcher 1904-07

JOHN J. "JACK" POWELL
pitcher 1904-05

JAMES COCKMAN
third baseman
1905

JOE YEAGER
shortstop 1905-06

1903
ROAD

1904
HOME

NEW YORK American League (continued)

The 1905 team in spring training. STANDING (L to R): Anderson, Chase, Hogg, Starkel, Chesbro, Puttman, Duff, Newton, Fultz, Dougherty, McGuire, Williams, Powell, Metcalf, Whiteley, Orth. SEATED: Martin (trainer), Griffith (mgr.), Clarkson, Keeler, Conroy, Kleinow, Yeager.

EUSTACE "DOC" NEWTON
pitcher 1905-09

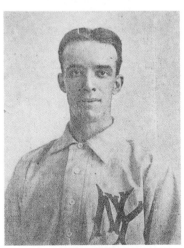

BILL HOGG
pitcher 1905-08

**1905
HOME**

DANNY HOFFMAN
outfielder 1906-07

ED HAHN
outfielder 1905-06

FRANK "POT" LAPORTE
utility 1905-07

FRANK DELAHANTY
first base, outfield
1905-06, 1908

NEW YORK American League (continued)

GEORGE MORIARTY
first, third base 1906-08

WESLEY "BRANCH" RICKEY
catcher, outfielder 1907

IRA THOMAS
catcher 1906-07

HAROLD "HAL" CHASE
first baseman 1905-09-

CORNELIUS "NEAL" BALL
shortstop 1907-09

JUDD "SLOW JOE" DOYLE
pitcher 1906-09-

**THOMAS L.
"SALIDA TOM" HUGHES**
pitcher 1906-09-

1908
ROAD

LEWIS "KING" BROCKETT
pitcher 1907, 1909

WALTER BLAIR
catcher 1907-09-

**WALTER S.
"RUBE" MANNING**
pitcher
1907-09-

NEW YORK American League (continued)

HARRY NILES
second baseman
1908

GARLAND "JAKE" STAHL
first base, outfield
1908

ED SWEENEY
catcher 1908-09-

CHARLES HEMPHILL
outfielder
1908-09-

JOE LAKE
pitcher
1908-09

CLYDE ENGLE
outfielder 1909-

WILLIAM F. "BIRDIE" CREE
outfielder 1908-09-

JACK WARHOP
pitcher 1908-09-

JAMES S. "QUEENIE" O'ROURKE
utility
1908

JOHN W. "JACK" KNIGHT
utility 1909-

JOHN "JACK" QUINN (PICUS)
pitcher 1909-

JIMMY AUSTIN
shortstop, third base
1909-

CHARLES "RAY" DEMMITT
outfielder 1909

1909
HOME

NEW YORK National League . . . . GIANTS

OWNERS & OFFICERS:

ANDREW FREEDMAN
owner, president
1900-02

JOHN T. BRUSH
owner, president
late 1902-09-

FRED KNOWLES
sec'y/treas.
1900-09-

CHARLES W. MURPHY
asst. sec'y/dir.

executive secretary: groundskeepers: trainer:
MARY SULLIVAN   **ARTHUR BELL**   **HARRY TUTHILL**
               MIKE MURPHY

directors:
E. B. TALCOTT   VALENTINE P. SNYDER
H. M. STEVENS   CORNELIUS SULLIVAN
N. ASHLEY LLOYD   THOMAS L. HAMILTON
A. C. ANSON   FRED KNOWLES
H. N. HEMPSTEAD   AUGUST BELMONT
MIKE TIERNAN
RICHARD CROKER
JOHN T. BRUSH

FIELD MANAGERS:

WILLIAM "BUCK" EWING
1900

GEORGE S. DAVIS
late 1900-1901

HORACE FOGEL
early 1902

GEORGE H. "HEINIE" SMITH
mid 1902

JOHN J. McGRAW
late 1902-1909-

THE PLAYERS:

NEW YORK National League (continued)

GEORGE S. "WIN" MERCER
pitcher, utility
1900

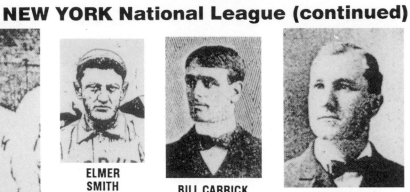

ELMER SMITH
outfielder
1900

BILL CARRICK
pitcher
1900

ALBERT K. "KIP" SELBACH
outfielder
1900-01

WILLIAM J. "KID" GLEASON
second baseman
1900

CHARLES "PIANO LEGS" HICKMAN
utility
1900-01

MIKE GRADY
catcher 1900

GEORGE VAN HALTREN
pitcher, outfielder 1900-03

JOHN J. "JACK" DOYLE
first baseman 1900, 1902

J. BENTLEY "CY" SEYMOUR
pitcher, outfielder
1900, 1906-09-

FRANK BOWERMAN
catcher 1900-07

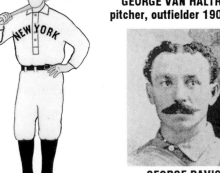

1900 HOME

GEORGE DAVIS
utility infielder
1900-01, 1903
(mgr. 1901, captain 1900-01)

NEW YORK National League (continued)

CHRISTY MATHEWSON
pitcher 1900-09-

ED DOHENY
pitcher 1900-01

JOHN "JACK" WARNER
catcher 1900-01, 1903-04

ALEXANDER
"BROADWAY ALEC"
SMITH
utility 1901, 1906

BILL PHYLE
pitcher 1901

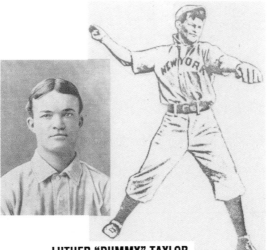

LUTHER "DUMMY" TAYLOR
pitcher 1900-08

ALGIE McBRIDE
outfielder 1901

1901
ROAD

RAYMOND "KELL" NELSON
second baseman 1901

JAMES T.
"SHERIFF" JONES
pitcher, outfield
1901-02

NEW YORK National League (continued)

**SAMMY STRANG
(NICKLIN)**
**third baseman
1901, 1905-08**

JOHN GANZELL
first baseman 1901

**GEORGE H.
"HEINIE" SMITH**
second base 1902
(mgr. 1902)
(captain 1902)

ROGER BRESNAHAN
catcher, utility 1902-08

JOHN McGRAW
utility 1902-06
(mgr. 1902-09)
(captain 1902-04)

JOSEPH "IRON MAN" JOE McGINNITY
pitcher 1902-08

HARRY O'HAGEN
first baseman 1902

**JAMES B.
"JIM" JACKSON**
**outfielder
1902**

JOSEPH W. BEAN
shortstop 1902

LEROY EVANS
pitcher 1902

**WALTER S.
"STEVE" BRODIE**
outfielder 1902

DAN McGANN
first baseman 1902-07
(captain 1905-07)

BILLY LAUDER
third baseman 1902-03

JACK DUNN
pitcher 1902-05

GEORGE BROWNE
outfielder
1902-07

JACK CRONIN
pitcher 1902-03

BILLY GILBERT
second baseman 1903-06

CHARLES BABB
shortstop 1903

**SAMUEL
"SANDOW" MERTES**
outfielder 1903-06

Secretary
FRED KNOWLES

The 1903 team. (L to R): McGraw (mgr.), Bresnahan, Lauder, Mertes, Taylor, Browne, McGann, McGinnity, (mascots), Warner, Van Haltren, Mathewson, Cronin, Ames, Babb, Dunn.

PHILADELPHIA National League (continued)

CHARLES "RED" DOOIN
catcher 1902-09-

CHARLES
"CHIEF" ZIMMER
catcher 1903
(mgr. 1903)

ROY BRASHEAR
second baseman
1903

JOHN TITUS
outfielder 1903-09-

THOMAS "TULLY" SPARKS
pitcher 1903-09-

JOHN "JACK" McFETRIDGE
pitcher 1903

BILL KEISTER
outfielder
1903

BOB HALL
infielder, utility
1904

JOHN
"JACK" SUTTHOFF
pitcher 1904-05

JOHN LUSH
pitcher, utility
1904-07

FRED MITCHELL
pitcher 1903-04

FRANK ROTH
catcher 1903-04

WILLIAM J.
"KID" GLEASON
second baseman 1903-08
(captain 1905-07)
(coach 1908-09)

JOHN McPHERSON
pitcher 1904

JOHN J.
"JACK" DOYLE
first baseman 1904

1904
ROAD

PHILADELPHIA National League (continued)

SHERWOOD "SHERRY" MAGEE
outfielder 1904-09-

FRANK CORRIDON
pitcher 1904-09

FRED ABBOTT
catcher 1905

OTTO KNABE
second baseman
1905-09-

ARTHUR W. "OTTO" KRUEGER
utility 1905

CHARLES A. "KID" NICHOLS
pitcher 1905-06

ERNIE COURTNEY
third baseman 1905-08

1906 HOME

MIKE DOOLAN
shortstop 1905-09-
(captain 1908-09)

CHARLES PITTINGER
pitcher 1905-07

WILLIAM E. "KITTY" BRANSFIELD
first baseman 1905-09-

EDWARD R. DOHENY
pitcher 1901-03

JIMMY BURKE
utility 1901-02

WILLIAM "KITTY" BRANSFIELD
first baseman 1901-04

WILLIAM "WID" CONROY
shortstop, outfield 1902

JIMMY SEBRING
outfielder 1902-04

EDWARD PHELPS
catcher 1902-04, 1906-08

HARRY SMITH
catcher 1902-07

**ARTHUR W.
"OTTO" KRUEGER**
utility 1903-04

ART WEAVER
catcher 1903

FRED CARISCH
catcher
1903-06

**HARRY E.
"MOOSE" McCORMICK**
outfielder 1904

**IRVIN K.
"KAISER" WILHELM**
pitcher 1903

**WILLIAM P.
"BRICKYARD" KENNEDY**
pitcher 1903

SAMUEL H. "HOWIE" CAMNITZ
pitcher 1904-09-

CHARLES CASE
pitcher 1904-06

1903
ROAD

PITTSBURGH National League (continued)

MIKE LYNCH
pitcher 1904-07

DAVE BRAIN
infielder 1905

GEORGE E. "DEL" HOWARD
first base, outfield
1905

OTIS CLYMER
outfielder 1905-07

ROSCOE MILLER
pitcher 1904

**HOMER
"DOC" HILLEBRAND**
pitcher 1905-06, 1908

HENRY "HEINIE" PEITZ
catcher 1905-06

BOB GANLEY
outfielder 1905-06

GEORGE GIBSON
catcher 1905-09–

WILLIAM E. CLANCEY
first baseman 1905

**1906
ROAD**

AL "LEFTY" LEIFIELD
pitcher 1905-09–

JIM NEALON
first baseman 1906-07

TOMMY SHEEHAN
third baseman 1906-07

WILLIAM H. HALLMAN
outfielder 1906-07

PITTSBURGH National League (continued)

VIC WILLIS
pitcher 1906-09

The 1907 team. TOP ROW (L to R): Gibson, Phelps, Lynch, Leifield, Willis, Nealon, Phillipe. MIDDLE: Leach, Hallman, Smith, Abbaticchio, Clymer. BOTTOM: Leever, Wagner, Clarke (mgr.), Brady, Anderson, Storke.

**ARTHUR E.
"DUTCH" MEIER**
utility 1906

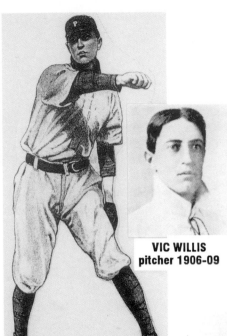

EDWARD "GOAT" ANDERSON
outfielder 1907

NICK MADDOX
pitcher 1907-09-

**ALAN
STORKE**
infielder
1906-09

HARRY SWACINA
first baseman 1907-08

1907
HOME

BILL ABSTEIN
first baseman 1906, 1909

ED ABBATICCHIO
second base, shortstop
1907-09-

PITTSBURGH National League (continued)

CHARLES "BABE" ADAMS
pitcher 1907-09-

JOHN OWEN "CHIEF" WILSON
outfielder 1908-09-

BOBBY BYRNE
third baseman
1909

PAT O'CONNOR
catcher
1908-09

1908
ROAD

ROY THOMAS
outfielder
1908

JOHN B. "DOTS" MILLER
second baseman 1909-

ROBERT H. "HAM" HYATT
outfielder 1909

1909
HOME

**WILLIAM J.
"JAP" BARBEAU**
third baseman 1909

ST. LOUIS American League . . . . RAVENS, BROWNS

OWNERS & OFFICERS:

**RALPH
ORTHWEIN
president
1902-03**

attorney 1902:
J. D. JOHNSON

**JOHN E.
BRUCE
attorney
1906-**

**ROBERT L. HEDGES
business mgr. 1902
secretary/treas. 1903
owner/president 1903-09-**

vice presidents:
**JAMES GHIO
BEN ADKINS**

secretaries:
**BILLY WALSH
SID MERCER
LLOYD RICKERT**

directors:
**LACEY CRAWFORD
RUSSELL D. GARDNER
BEN ADKINS
FRED HIRSCH
ANTON STEUER
J. C. McDIARMID**

FIELD MANAGER:

**JAMES McALEER
1902-1909**

**1902
ROAD**

1904

THE PLAYERS:

**CHARLES HEMPHILL
outfielder 1902-07**

**EMMET HEIDRICK
outfielder 1902-04, 08**

**JOHN
"JIGGS" DONAHUE
catcher, first base
1902**

**JOHN
ANDERSON
first baseman
1902-03**

**JOE SUGDEN
catcher, utility
1902-05**

ST. LOUIS American League (continued)

JESS BURKETT
outfielder 1902-04

DICK PADDEN
second baseman
1902-05
(captain 1902-05)

MIKE KAHOE
catcher 1902-04

BARRY McCORMICK
utility 1902-03

BOBBY WALLACE
shortstop
1902-09-

CHARLES W.
"JACK" HARPER
pitcher 1902

JOHN J.
"JACK," "RED" POWELL
pitcher, utility
1902-03, 1905-09-

BILL FRIEL
utility 1902-03

FRANK "RED" DONAHUE
pitcher 1902-03

ST. LOUIS American League (continued)

BILL REIDY
pitcher, utility
1902-03

**JOHN W.
"WILLIE" SUDHOFF**
pitcher 1902-05

JOE MARTIN
utility 1903

**CLARENCE
EUGENE WRIGHT**
pitcher
1903-04

ED SIEVER
pitcher 1903-04

HUNTER HILL
third baseman
1903-04

BARNEY PELTY
pitcher
1903-09-

**ED "PINKY"
SWANDER**
outfielder
1903-04

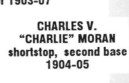

**HARRY R.
"CY" MORGAN**
pitcher 1903-07

**CHARLES V.
"CHARLIE" MORAN**
shortstop, second base
1904-05

PAT HYNES
pitcher, outfield
1904

ST. LOUIS American League (continued)

TOM JONES
first baseman
1904-09

JACK O'CONNOR
catcher
1904-09-
(captain 1906-08)

HENRY "HARRY" HOWELL
pitcher 1904-09-

FRED GLADE
pitcher 1904-07

HARRY GLEASON
utility 1904-05

CHARLES STARR
second baseman
1905

ART WEAVER
catcher
1905

BEN KOEHLER
outfielder
1905-06

JOHN "EMIL" FRISK
outfielder
1905, 1907

ST. LOUIS American League (continued)

IKE ROCKENFIELD
second baseman
1905-06

JAMES BUCHANAN
pitcher 1905

**CHARLES
"IKE" VAN ZANDT**
outfielder
1905

PETE O'BRIEN
second, third base
1906

GEORGE STONE
outfielder
1905-09-

**LOUIS
NORDYKE**
first baseman
1906

**EDWARD R.
"TUBBY" SPENCER**
catcher 1905-08

**WESLEY
BRANCH RICKEY**
catcher 1905-06

1906
HOME

The 1906 team. TOP ROW (L to R): Buchanan, Morgan, Smith, Stone, Jones, Spencer. MIDDLE: Powell, Glade, Jacobson, Rickey, Niles, Hemphill, O'Brien, Koehler. BOTTOM: Pelty, O'Connor, Howell, Nordyke, Hartzell, Wallace.

ST. LOUIS American League (continued)

ALBERT "BEANY" JACOBSON
pitcher 1906-07

BILL DINNEEN
pitcher 1907-09

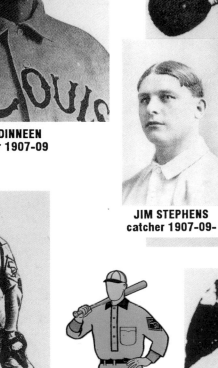

ROY HARTZELL
utility 1906-09–

JIM STEPHENS
catcher 1907-09–

JIM DELAHANTY
infielder 1907

HARRY NILES
utility 1906-07

RHESA "ED" SMITH
pitcher 1906

1907 HOME

FRED "FRITZ" BUELOW
catcher 1907

OLLIE PICKERING
outfielder 1907

WILLIS "KID" BUTLER
third base 1907

1907 ROAD

JOE YEAGER
infielder 1907-08

ST. LOUIS American League (continued)

BILL BAILEY
pitcher 1907-09-

**ALBERT
"HOBE" FERRIS**
infielder 1908-09

CHARLES "CASEY" JONES
outfielder 1908

WILLIAM GRAHAM
pitcher 1908-09-

AL SCHWEITZER
outfielder 1908-09-

**1908
HOME**

JIMMY WILLIAMS
second baseman
1908-09

DANNY HOFFMAN
outfielder 1908

The 1908 team. TOP ROW (L to R): Stephens, Blue, Waddell, Dinneen, T. Jones, Yeager, Williams. MIDDLE: O'Connor, Schweitzer, C. Jones, Stone, Hoffman, Spencer, Bailey. SEATED: Wallace, Pelty, Howell, McAleer (mgr.), Hartzell, Powell, Ferris.

ST. LOUIS American League (continued)

GEORGE E. "RUBE" WADDELL
pitcher 1908-09-

DODE CRISS
pitcher, outfielder 1908-09-

ART GRIGGS
first base, outfield 1909-

JOHN "JACK" McALEESE
outfielder 1909

1909 ROAD

BURT SHOTTON
outfielder 1909-

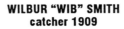

WILBUR "WIB" SMITH
catcher 1909

LOU CRIGER
catcher 1909

ST. LOUIS National League . . . . .CARDINALS

OWNERS & OFFICERS:

FRANK DeHAAS ROBISON
owner, president 1900-06
(died in 1908)

MATTHEW STANLEY ROBISON
vice president, treasurer:
1900-06
president:
1907-09-

secretaries:
LOUIS HEILBRONER
WM. W. SCHOFIELD
LOUIS SEEKAMP

bus. mgr. 1904:
H. S. MUCKENFOSS

E. A. STEININGER

directors:
EDW. C. BECKER
HENRY NICOLAS
PATSY TEBEAU

FIELD MANAGERS:

OLIVER "PATSY" TEBEAU
1900

LOUIS HEILBRONER
late 1900

PATRICK "PATSY" DONOVAN
1901-1903

CHARLES "KID" NICHOLS
1904-early 1905

JIMMY BURKE
mid 1905

M. STANLEY ROBISON
late 1905

JOHN McCLOSKEY
1906-1908

ROGER BRESNAHAN
1909

ST. LOUIS National League (continued)

THE PLAYERS:

The 1900 team. TOP ROW (L to R): Schreckengost, Jones, Young, Donovan, Knepper, Harper. MIDDLE: Powell, Wallace, Heidrick, Burkett, Donlin, Tebeau (mgr.), Buelow, Criger, McGann, Dillard. BOTTOM: O'Connor, Keister, Cuppy, Cross, Hughey.

DENTON T. "CY" YOUNG
pitcher 1900

JIM HUGHEY
pitcher 1900

JOHN McGRAW
third baseman 1900
(captain 1900)

WILBERT ROBINSON
catcher 1900

BOBBY WALLACE
shortstop 1900-01

CHARLES W. "JACK" HARPER
pitcher 1900-01

ST. LOUIS National League (continued)

JACK O'CONNOR
catcher 1900

**LAFAYETTE NAPOLEON
"LAVE" CROSS**
third baseman 1900

**ROBERT L.
"PAT" DILLARD**
third base, outfield
1900

**LOU
CRIGER**
catcher
1900

BILL KEISTER
second baseman
1900

**AUGUSTUS "GUS"
WEYHING**
pitcher
1900

**PATSY
DONOVAN**
outfielder
1900-03
_(mgr.
1901-03)
(captain
1900-?)_

JOE QUINN
infielder 1900

TOM THOMAS
pitcher 1900

WILLIE SUDHOFF
pitcher 1900-01

MIKE DONLIN
first baseman 1900

JESSE BURKETT
outfielder 1900-01

**JOHN J. "JACK"
"RED" POWELL**
pitcher 1900-01

DAN McGANN
first baseman
1900-01

EMMET HEIDRICK
outfielder 1900-01

**ALBERT E.
"BURT" JONES**
pitcher 1900-01

ST. LOUIS National League (continued)

ARTHUR W. "OTTO" KRUEGER
infielder 1900-02

STAN YERKES
pitcher
1901-03

EDWARD J. MURPHY
pitcher 1901-03

BILLY MALONEY
catcher, outfielder
1902

MIKE O'NEILL
pitcher 1901-04

GEORGE BARCLAY
outfielder 1902-04

1903
HOME

FRED HARTMAN
infielder 1902

WILLIAM F. "POP" SCHRIVER
catcher 1901

BOB WICKER
pitcher, outfielder
1901-03

JOHN B. "JACK" RYAN
catcher, infielder
1901-03

ART NICHOLS
catcher, utility 1901-03

DICK PADDEN
second baseman 1901

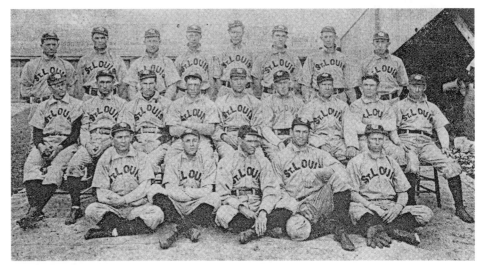

The 1903 team. TOP ROW (L to R): Smith, Murphy, McFarland, Weaver, Hackett, Milton, Yerkes, Smoot. MIDDLE: Wicker, Brain, Rhoades, J. O'Neill, Donovan (mgr.), Burke, Ryan, Farrell, Nichols. BOTTOM: Barclay, Williams, Sanders, M. O'Neill, Brown.

NORMAN C. "KITTY" BRASHEAR
utility 1902

ART WEAVER
catcher 1902-03

CLARENCE CURRIE
pitcher
1902-03

OTTO WILLIAMS
utility
1902-03

JAMES HACKETT
pitcher, outfielder
1902-03

**JOHN J.
"JACK" O'NEILL**
catcher 1902-03

JOHN S. FARRELL
second baseman
1902-05

**CHARLES
"CHAPPIE" McFARLAND**
pitcher 1902-06

HOMER SMOOT
outfielder
1902-06

WARREN SANDERS
pitcher 1903-04

ROBERT "DUSTY" RHOADES
pitcher 1903

ST. LOUIS National League (continued)

MORDECAI BROWN
pitcher 1903

JAMES DUNLEAVY
pitcher, outfielder
1903-05

DAVE BRAIN
infielder 1903-05
(captain 1905)

**JOHN B.
"LARRY" McLEAN**
catcher 1904

DAVID ZEARFOSS
catcher 1904-05

JOE CORBETT
pitcher 1904

JAKE BECKLEY
first baseman 1904-07
(captain 1904)

**WILLIAM P.
"SPIKE" SHANNON**
outfielder
1904-06

JIMMY BURKE
second base, third base
1903-05
(mgr., mid 1905)

DANNY SHAY
shortstop, second baseman
1904-05

1906
HOME

1906
ROAD

ST. LOUIS National League (continued)

**CHARLES A.
"KID" NICHOLS**
pitcher 1904-05
(mgr. 1904-05)

**JOHN W.
"JACK" TAYLOR**
pitcher 1904-06

MIKE GRADY
**catcher, first baseman
1904-06**

TOM LEAHY
**catcher
1905**

JOSHUA "JOSH" CLARKE
outfielder 1905

**JOHN
"JACK"
WARNER**
**catcher
1905**

The 1905 team. STANDING (L to R): Brain, Hill, Taylor, McFarland, Egan, Burch, Smoot, Warner, McGinley, Thielman, Grady. SEATED: Dunleavy, Butler, Kellum, Clarke, Zearfoss, Nichols (mgr.), Campbell, Farrell, Burke, Shannon.

ST. LOUIS National League (continued)

HARRY ARNDT
Infielder 1905-07

GEORGE McBRIDE
shortstop
1905-06

**ALOYSIUS
"WISH" EGAN**
pitcher 1905-06

JOHN P. "JAKE" THIELMAN
pitcher 1905-06

**JOHN G.
"GUS" THOMPSON**
pitcher 1906

JOE MARSHALL
outfielder 1906

**SAMUEL
"SANDOW" MERTES**
outfielder 1906

**JUSTIN N.
"PUG" BENNETT**
second baseman
1906-07

**JOHN C.
"SHAD" BARRY**
utility
1906-08
(captain 1908)

**CHARLES E.
"BUSTER" BROWN**
pitcher 1905-07

**ART
HOSTETTER
(HOELSKOETTER)**
pitcher, utility
1905-08

AL BURCH
outfielder 1906-07

FRED BEEBE
pitcher 1906-09

**FORREST
CRAWFORD**
shortstop
1906-07

ST. LOUIS National League (continued)

ED HOLLY shortstop 1906-07

PETE NOONAN
catcher
1906-07

ED KARGER
pitcher 1906-08

JOHN "RED" MURRAY
outfielder 1906-08

TOM O'HARA
outfielder 1906-07

WILLIAM R.
"DOC" MARSHALL
catcher
1906-08

IRVING HIGGINBOTHAM
pitcher 1906-09

ULYSSES S. G.
"STONEY" McGLYNN
pitcher 1906-08

ART FROMME
pitcher 1906-08

JOHN B. KELLY
outfielder 1907

JOHN P.
BURNETT
outfielder
1907

ST. LOUIS National League (continued)

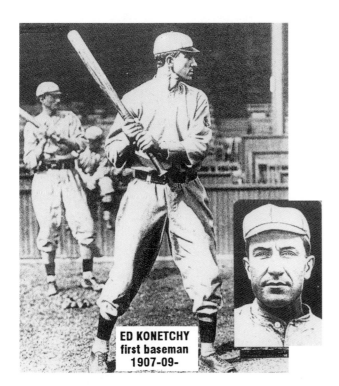

JOE DELAHANTY
outfielder
1907-09

ALBERT S. SHAW
outfielder
1907-09

BILLY GILBERT
second baseman
1908-09

JOSEPH L. "PATSY" O'ROURKE
shortstop
1908

ED KONETCHY
first baseman
1907-09-

WILBUR MURDOCK
outfielder 1908

BILL LUDWIG
catcher
1908

RAYMOND "CHAPPY" CHARLES
infielder 1908-09

BOBBY BYRNE
third baseman
1907-09

ARTHUR "BUGS" RAYMOND
pitcher 1907-08

JOHN LUSH
pitcher 1907-09-

HARRY F. "SLIM" SALLEE
pitcher 1908-09-

ST. LOUIS National League (continued)

JOHN J. "JACK" BLISS
catcher 1908-09-

RUDY HULSWITT
shortstop 1909

ED PHELPS catcher 1909-

BOB HARMON pitcher 1909-

GEORGE "RUBE" ELLIS
outfielder 1909-

LOUIS "STEVE" EVANS
outfielder 1909-

ROGER BRESNAHAN
catcher 1909-
(manager 1909-)
(captain 1909)

ALAN STORKE
shortstop
1909

**WILLIAM J.
"JAP" BARBEAU**
third baseman
1909

1909
HOME

WASHINGTON American League . . . . SENATORS, NATIONALS

OWNERS & OFFICERS:

FRED POSTAL
president
1901-03

TOM LOFTUS
president
1904

vice president:
EUGÉNE COCHRAN

V.P./treasurer:
WM. J. DWYER

treasurer:
WM. FOWLER
? RAPLEY

secretary:
JOHN WALSH
BEN S. MINOR
WM. FOWLER

trainer:
JERRY EDINGER

groundskeeper:
MILLER
O'DAY
ADMIRAL BROWN
? NEWHOUSE

vice president:
JAMES MANNING
CHARLES JACOBSON

secretary:
BO NEEDHAM 1901
CLARK POTTER 1902
WALTER HEWETT 1903

directors:
TOM LOFTUS
JAMES MANNING
JOHN J. HOGAN
WILLIAM HART
JOHN R. McLEAN
JAMES WADSWORTH
W. C. BRYAN
WM. DONOVAN
WILTON J. LAMBERT

THOMAS NOYES
president 1905-09

directors:
HENRY L. WEST
SCOTT BONE
G. HECTOR CLEMES
MICHAEL SCANLON
FRANK HISS
B. F. MORRIS

FIELD MANAGERS:

JIMMY MANNING
1901

TOM LOFTUS
1902-1903

MALACHI
KITTRIDGE
early 1904
(acting manager)

PATSY DONOVAN
1904

1901
HOME

JAKE STAHL
1905-1906

JOE CANTILLON
1907-1909

WASHINGTON American League (continued)

THE PLAYERS:

MIKE GRADY
catcher, first baseman
1901

**WILLIAM
"BOILERYARD" CLARKE**
catcher 1901-04
(captain 1901)

BILLY CLINGMAN
shortstop
1901

WILLIAM EVERETT
first baseman 1901
(captain 1901)

JOE QUINN
second baseman 1901

JOHN "JACK" O'BRIEN
outfielder 1901

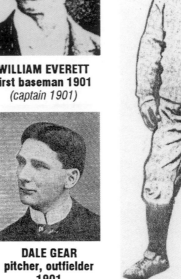

BILL COUGHLIN
third baseman 1901-04

DALE GEAR
pitcher, outfielder
1901

JOHN S. FARRELL
second base, outfield 1901

GEORGE "WIN" MERCER
pitcher 1901

The 1901 team. STANDING (L to R): Dungan, Patten, Everett, O'Brien, Coughlin, Clarke, Farrell, Gear, Grady.
KNEELING: Quinn, Lee, (?), Carrick, Clingman.

SAM DUNGAN
first base, outfield
1901

IRV WALDRON
outfielder 1901

**CLARENCE F.
"POP" FOSTER**
outfielder 1901

WASHINGTON American League (continued)

BILL CARRICK
pitcher 1901-02

CASE PATTEN
pitcher 1901-08

JOHN J. "JACK" DOYLE
utility 1902

HARRY WOLVERTON
third baseman 1902

WYATT "WATTY" LEE
pitcher, outfielder 1901-03

1902
ROAD

LEW DRILL
catcher, utility 1902-04

JIMMY RYAN
outfielder 1902-03
(captain 1902)

GEORGE "SCOOPS" CAREY
first baseman
1902-03

ED DELAHANTY
first baseman, outfielder 1902-03

FRED "BONES" ELY
shortstop 1902

BILL KEISTER
utility 1902

JOHN "JACK" TOWNSEND
pitcher 1902-05

AL ORTH
pitcher, utility 1902-04

"BARRY" McCORMICK
second baseman 1902-03

WASHINGTON American League (continued)

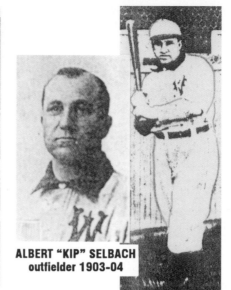

ALBERT "KIP" SELBACH
outfielder 1903-04

HOWARD P.
"HIGHBALL" WILSON
pitcher 1903-04

The 1903 team. TOP ROW (L to R): Delahanty, Selbach, Orth, Carey, Patten, Townsend, Moran. MIDDLE: Clarke, Lee, Loftus (mgr.), Coughlin, Martin, Ryan. BOTTOM: Holmes, Robinson, DeMontreville, Drill.

JOE MARTIN
utility 1903

JOHN HENDRICKS
outfielder 1903

1903
HOME

JAMES W.
"DUCKY" HOLMES
utility 1903

EDWARD P.
"DAVEY" DUNKLE
pitcher 1903-04

CLYDE ROBINSON
utility 1903

CHARLIE MORAN
shortstop 1903-04

MALACHI
KITTRIDGE
catcher 1903-06
(acting mgr., captain 1904)

WASHINGTON American League (continued)

PATSY DONOVAN
outfielder *(mgr.)* 1904
(captain 1904)

WILLIAM WOLFE
pitcher 1904-06

**ALBERT
"BEANY" JACOBSON**
pitcher 1904-05

HUNTER HILL
third baseman
1904-05

JOE CASSIDY
utility
1904-05

FRANK E. HUELSMAN
outfielder 1904-05

THOMAS "LONG TOM" HUGHES
pitcher 1904-09-

**WILLIAM J.
"BILL" O'NEILL**
outfielder 1904

**JIM
MULLIN**
second base
1904-05

**CHARLES E.
"PUNCH" KNOLL**
outfielder 1905

**1905
HOME**

GARLAND "JAKE" STAHL
first base, outfield 1904-06
(manager, captain 1905-06)

WASHINGTON American League (continued)

CHARLES HICKMAN
first base, utility
1905-07

MIKE HEYDON
catcher
1905-07

**CHARLES "CHARLIE"
"CASEY" JONES**
outfielder 1905-07

HOWARD WAKEFIELD
catcher 1906

DAVE ALTIZER
utility 1906-08

**GEORGE C.
"RABBIT" NILL**
utility 1904-07

**LAFAYETTE
NAPOLEON
"LAVE" CROSS**
third baseman
1906-07

LARRY SCHLAFLY
second base 1906-07
(captain 1907)

1906
ROAD

JOE STANLEY
outfielder
1905-06

JOHN "JACK" WARNER
catcher 1906-08

BOB EDMONDSON
pitcher, outfielder
1906, 1908

JOHN ANDERSON
first base, outfield
1905-07

FRED "CY" FALKENBURG
pitcher 1905-08

FRANK KITSON
pitcher
1906-07

WASHINGTON American League (continued)

The 1907 team. TOP ROW (L to R): Smith, Stanage, Falkenburg, Heydon, Eddinger (trainer), Anderson, Hughes, Graham. MIDDLE: Nill, Jones, Warner, Cantillon (mgr.), Cross, Hickman, Perrine, Schlafly. BOTTOM: Kitson, Patten, Blankenship, Ganley.

CHARLEY SMITH
pitcher 1906-09

MIKE KAHOE
catcher 1907-09

JAMES "BRUNO" BLOCK
catcher 1907

TONY SMITH
shortstop 1907

PETE O'BRIEN
second baseman 1907

JOHN "NIG" PERRINE
utility infield 1907

WALTER KAY
outfielder 1907

OSCAR GRAHAM
pitcher 1907

1907
ROAD

FRANK OBERLIN
pitcher 1907, 1909

WASHINGTON American League (continued)

WALTER JOHNSON
pitcher 1907-09-

BOB GANLEY
outfielder 1907-09
(captain 1908-09)

OTIS CLYMER
outfielder
1907-09

CLIFF BLANKENSHIP
catcher 1907, 1909

BILL SHIPKE
third baseman 1907-09

JIM DELAHANTY
infielder 1907-09

HENRY GEHRING
pitcher 1907-08

WASHINGTON American League (continued)

JESSE CLYDE "DEERFOOT" MILAN
outfielder
1907-09-

JESS TANNEHILL
pitcher 1908-09

FRANK "JERRY" FREEMAN
first baseman 1908-09

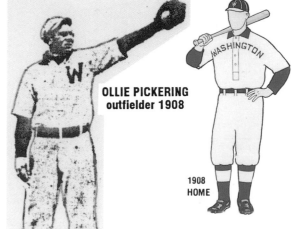

OLLIE PICKERING
outfielder 1908

1908
HOME

BOB UNGLAUB
first base,
utility
1908-09-

The 1908 team. BACK ROW, STANDING (L to R): Ganley, Cates, Edmondson, Johnson, Witherup, Hughes, Clymer, Pickering, McBride. MIDDLE, SEATED: Smith, Freeman, Milan, Cantillon (mgr.), Tannehill, Delahanty, Street. IN FRONT: Kahoe, Schipke.

ELI CATES
pitcher 1908

WASHINGTON American League (continued)

BILL BURNS
pitcher 1908-09

1909 HOME

GEORGE McBRIDE
shortstop 1908-09-

BURT KEELEY
pitcher 1908-09

1909 ROAD

HARRY "DOC" GESSLER
outfield 1909-

NICK ALTROCK
pitcher 1909-

CHARLES "GABBY" STREET
catcher 1908-09-

HERMAN "GERMANY" SCHAEFER
second base 1909-

JOHN F. "JACK" LELIVELT
outfielder 1909-

WILLIAM "WID" CONROY
third baseman 1909-

"JIGGS" DONAHUE
first baseman 1909

WILLIAM "DOLLY" GRAY
pitcher 1909-

GEORGE BROWNE
outfielder 1909

WADE "RED" KILLEFER
second base 1909-

BOB GROOM
pitcher 1909-

1900

BOER WAR RAGES IN SOUTH AFRICA

HAWAII BECOMES U.S. TERRITORY

BOXER REBELLION IN CHINA

PARIS HOSTS OLYMPIC GAMES

SUCCESSFUL FLIGHT OF 1ST DIRIGIBLE

McKINLEY RE-ELECTED, ROOSEVELT NEW VICE PRESIDENT

U.S. POPULATION 76 MILLION

NYC SUBWAY BEGUN

STORM RAVAGES GALVESTON

CASEY JONES DIES IN TRAIN WRECK

FIRST DAVIS CUP IN TENNIS

HARRY VARDON WINS U.S. OPEN

JEFFRIES DEFEATS CORBETT

The baseball world of 1900 was stunned in January by the tragic death of Boston's Marty Bergen, who took his own life after killing his wife and children. Perhaps an ominous beginning of the new century for the pared-down NL circuit of eight teams. After a fairly prosperous and reasonably peaceful eight-year period of an unchallenged 12-team major league alignment, the National League was troubled by bickering owners and an unsavory public image. The rosters of the four disenfranchised clubs (Cleveland, Louisville, Baltimore, Washington) had already been shamefully drained off by some of the stronger clubs in 1899. Attendance was down and rowdyism was up. The oligarchy of headstrong, independent owners held loosely together by a National Agreement and governed by a largely impotent league president resulted in an uneasy situation for big league baseball. Ban Johnson's Western League had renamed itself the American League and signed on many of the reserves cast adrift by the reduced major league player pool. Cleveland quickly joined the new circuit and Charles Comiskey was permitted to transfer his St. Paul franchise to the south side of Chicago as a minor league operation. It was a prelude to more significant developments in 1901.

Austerity was the prevalent theme for major league baseball in 1900. Down to eight clubs, that meant a maximum of four games on any given day, thus only four full time umpires on the National League payroll since a single umpire officiated each game. The schedule was also reduced to 140 games. The traditional square home plate was redesigned into the five-sided shape of today. The wholesale reduction of available positions on ML clubs resulted in the formation of a new players union—the Protective Association of Professional Baseball Players—with Charles "Chief" Zimmer named as president.

Boston catcher Marty Bergen, who took his own life after that of his wife and children.

Ban Johnson renamed his Western League the American League and made plans to go "major" in 1901.

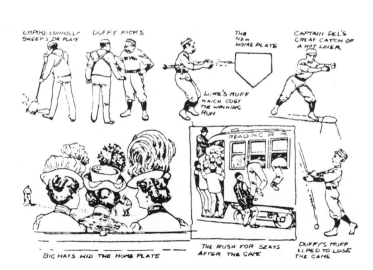

A St. Louis Post-Dispatch cartoonist's view of a Cardinals' game in 1900.

A Philadelphia newspaper's cartoon impressions of the 1900 home opener.

Another Philadelphia newspaper artist's interpretation of opening day 1900.

1900 (continued)

A newspaper artist sketched Manager Patsy Donovan accepting a floral good luck piece at the opener in St. Louis.

The Brooklyn club, its roster bolstered by the absorption of the best players from the defunct Baltimore team, won the league championship. Manager Ned Hanlon, included among the Baltimore transplants, happened to share a common last name with the leader of a popular circus act of the time called Hanlon's Superbas—resulting in a new nickname for the team. A glance at the Brooklyn roster also illustrates the predominance of Irish names in the game in 1900: DUNN, KELLEY, McGUIRE, McGINNITY, JENNINGS, DONOVAN, DALY. They finished 4-1/2 games ahead of a strong Pittsburgh club which had also inherited numerous star players from the former NL franchise in Louisville. Along with player/manager Fred Clarke and outfielder Tommy Leach, a locally born infielder named Honus Wagner emerged as Pittsburgh's new baseball hero. Wagner won his first of seven NL batting championships, hitting a rousing .381 and leading in doubles and triples. The St. Louis club, despite five future Hall-of-Famers on their roster, finished in the second division. The New York Giants brought up the rear. The top pitchers were Brooklyn's Joe McGinnity with 29 wins and Chicago's Rube Waddell with 133 strikeouts. On July 12, Cincinnati's "Noodles" Hahn tossed the only no-hit game of the 1900 season.

In the up-and-coming American League, Comiskey's Chicago White Stockings "brought home the bunting," or won the pennant as we would say it today.

A post-season series between champion Brooklyn and runner-up Pittsburgh was won by the Superbas, leaving no doubt about their claim to baseball supremacy.

Charles "Chief" Zimmer was named president of the new Players' Association.

Honus Wagner, a Pittsburgh area boy, joined the Pirates from the defunct Louisville club in 1900 and won the league batting title.

Cincinnati's Frank "Noodles" Hahn authored the league's only no-hitter for 1900.

Joe McGinnity gave the Brooklyns 29 victories on their way to a second straight flag in 1900.

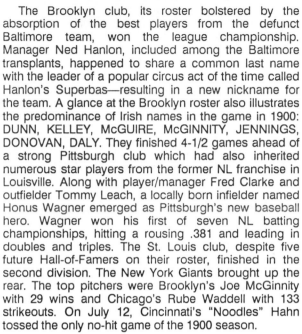

Opening day at Brooklyn's Washington Park. Cy Seymour of the visiting New Yorks is limbering up in the foreground.

Shannon's 23rd Regiment band leads the parade of the champion Superbas and the visiting Giants at the 1900 Brooklyn opener.

1901

PRES. McKINLEY ASSASSINATED
ROOSEVELT NEW PRESIDENT

QUEEN VICTORIA DEAD

FIRST NOBEL PRIZES AWARDED

WIRELESS SIGNAL CROSSES
ATLANTIC OCEAN

LAND RUSH IN OKLAHOMA

"SPINDLETOP" OIL DISCOVERY
IN TEXAS

PAN-AMERICAN EXPOSITION
IN BUFFALO

COLUMBIA WINS AMERICA'S CUP

ANDERSON WINS U.S. OPEN

JOE GANS WINS LIGHTWEIGHT
CHAMPIONSHIP

The year began with the untimely death of Pittsburgh utility player Tom O'Brien from pneumonia in February.

Following Ban Johnson's proclamation that his American League was now a major league, 1901 was to be the most eventful year of the decade. The structure of big league baseball was severely tested and all-out war was declared with the new rivals. The baseball map was altered forever. The National Agreement was undermined as established old league players jumped their contracts to sign on with the American League. The National League was in a state of chaos, especially in those cities (Boston, Chicago, St. Louis) forced to share their turf with the newcomers. In an attempt to shore up their defenses against the incursions of the invaders, the National League replaced president Nick Young with a triumvirate of club owners John T. Brush, Arthur A. Soden, and James Hart. Young was retained as secretary to the newly formed troika. Despite setbacks in the courts and embarrassing losses in attendance, the battle lines were drawn. The war entered the courts as attempts were unsuccessfully made to prohibit key players from defecting, notably Philadelphia's Nap Lajoie, Chick Fraser, and Bill Bernhard. For the most part, the American League was the early winner as established stars Cy Young, Jimmy Collins, John McGraw, Wilbert Robinson and Clark Griffith jumped aboard the American's bandwagon. The administrative genius of Ban Johnson along with the financial backing of wealthy magnates such as Charles Somers, Comiskey, and Ben Shibe gave the new venture early successes at the gate, generally outdrawing the old league clubs.

Napoleon Lajoie was at the center of a legal "firestorm" during the bitter AL vs. NL battles of 1901.

Pittsburgh's Tom O'Brien died suddenly in early 1901 at age 27.

THE NORTH AMERICAN, PHILADELPHIA, THURSDAY, MARCH 21, 1901.   15

THIRTY STAR PLAYERS HAVE BOLTED THE NATIONAL LEAGUE TO JOIN THE AMERICAN AND MORE HAVE PROMISED TO FOLLOW

F. DeH. Robinson.   Barney Dreyfus.   A. H. Soden.   Col. Jno. I. Rodgers.   Andrew Freedman.   James A. Hart.   J. T. Brush.   Charles H. Ebbets.

HOW THE OLD LEAGUE MAGNATES RECEIVED THE ANNOUNCEMENT

The threat of the emerging American League was front page "fodder" for the newspapers.

The new American League park in Philadelphia rapidly nearing completion in early 1901.

The Chicago White Stockings of the fledgling AL proudly display their 1900 championship pennant, about to be raised at the 1901 opener.

1901 (continued)

The unruly behavior that stained the game's image in 1900 was held in check by Ban Johnson's strict disciplinary controls which regained respect and won new fan support. Arguments, ejections, fines, and outright brawls (especially involving Baltimore's feisty manager McGraw) were still a part of the game but Johnson was able to keep a lid on it and assert the league's authority. Along with McGraw's ongoing feuds with umpires and league president Johnson, Milwaukee manager Hugh Duffy was suspended over a squabble with umpires. Johnson's iron fist came down hardest on Frank Shugart of Chicago, who was suspended for striking an umpire and never played again in the majors. The controversial new foul strike rule, intended to speed up the games, was introduced in the senior league.

Pittsburgh emerged as the new dynasty in the Senior Circuit replacing Brooklyn as league champions, Hans Wagner hit .352 and stole 48 bases while young Jack Chesbro won 21 for the pennant winners. Jess Burkett of St. Louis was the batting champ at .382, while Cincinnati's young outfielder Sam Crawford pounded out 16 home runs. The Reds' Noodles Hahn struck out 237 batters and the Bucknell graduate Mathewson of the NY Giants blossomed as a premier hurler, winning 20 games including a no-hitter on July 15.

Chicago's White Stockings, led by pitcher/manager Clark Griffith, repeated as American League champions and outdrew the crosstown NL Orphans at the turnstiles. The Athletics' Napoleon Lajoie tore up the new league with a .422 batting average. Portly hurler Cy Young celebrated his first year as a Boston American by winning 31 games and fanning 163.

THE AMERICAN LEAGUE SEASON OPENING AT BENNETT PARK TODAY.

A newspaper artist sketched the 1901 opener at Detroit's Bennett Park.

Christy Mathewson became a Polo Grounds favorite in 1901 with 20 victories and a no-hitter.

Cardinals' veteran Jess Burkett, a future Hall-of-Famer, claimed the 1901 NL batting title.

The astonishing total of 16 home runs came off the bat of Cincinnati's Sam Crawford.

Detroit first baseman Frank Dillon was one of the batting heroes in a remarkable ninth inning rally that resulted in an opening game victory over Milwaukee.

Mathewson on the mound in an April 1901 game in New York.

Giants' first baseman John Ganzell in action at a Polo Grounds contest.

The cartoonists around the American League cities had a field day with popular Baltimore stars Wilbert Robinson and John McGraw and their outragous road uniforms.

1902

MICHIGAN WINS FIRST ROSE BOWL
MT. PELEE VOLCANO ERUPTS
OLIVER WENDELL HOLMES NAMED CHIEF JUSTICE
EDWARD II CROWNED
FIRST HAGUE CONFERENCE
BOER WAR SETTLED
AUTOMOBILE CLUB OF AMERICA FORMED—23,000 AUTOS IN U.S.
BRET HARTE DEAD
FUNDS APPROVED FOR PANAMA CANAL PROJECT
EMILE ZOLA DIES
NATIONAL COAL STRIKE
FIRST CADILLAC AUTO MADE
FIRST RADIO TELEPHONE

The baseball wars with the rival AL were in full swing. The National League was in a state of near anarchy. A. G. Spalding was named president but the trio of Brush, Soden and Hart were still calling the shots. The American League was making significant inroads as more established NL players crossed over. The Milwaukee franchise was transferred to St. Louis and many of the Cardinal stars immediately came over to the Browns. The defection of Bobby Wallace, Jess Burkett, Dick Padden, Emmett Heidrick, Jack Harper and John Powell doomed the NL Cardinals to second division mediocrity for the balance of the decade. The old league finally won a victory in the Pennsylvania Supreme Court when Lajoie, Fraser and Bernhard were forbidden by injunction to play for the AL in Philadelphia. Fraser returned to the Phillies, but Lajoie and Bernhard were transferred by the AL to Cleveland, where they could legally play as long as they avoided playing dates in Philadelphia.

John McGraw became more and more of a liability to the Americans in Baltimore as he continually quarreled with the umpires and Ban Johnson. The team floundered as the season went on and, in a bizarre secret maneuver, the National League bought controlling interest in the Oriole franchise—a deal orchestrated by John T. Brush and Andy Freedman. As part of the arrangement, McGraw resigned in mid-season and signed on with the Giants, taking many of his key players with him (McGinnity, Bresnahan, McGann). Wilbert Robinson stayed behind and managed to salvage the rest of the season with a makeshift roster. But following Milwaukee, the Baltimores were destined to find a new home city the following year.

AMERICAN LEAGUE OPENS.

FIRST GAME OF NEW BROWNS AT SPORTSMAN'S PARK.

LEGAL TANGLE IN SIGHT.

National League May Bring Injunction Suit to Restrain Crack Players from Performing.

WHERE THE TEAMS PLAY.
CLEVELAND AT ST. LOUIS.
DETROIT AT CHICAGO.
PHILADELPHIA AT BALTIMORE.
BOSTON AT WASHINGTON.
LINE-UP HERE.

Browns.	Cleveland
Burkett, l. f.	Pickering, c. f.
Heidrick, c. f.	McCarthy, l. f.
Jones, r. f.	Harvey, r. f.
Anderson, 1b.	Shreckengost, 1b.
Wallace, ss.	Bonner, 2b.
Padden, 2b.	Bradley, 3b.
McCormick, 3b.	Gochnaur, ss.
Sugden, c.	Bemis, c.
Donahue, p.	Moore, p.

St. Louis joined the American League for 1902, taking over the Milwaukee franchise. They resurrected the old BROWNS nickname and promptly lured many star players from their neighboring NL club, the Cardinals.

Pittsburgh and Cincinnati players joined in hoisting the 1901 championship flag at the 1902 Exposition Park opener.

The American League pennant for the 1901 campaign once again flies proudly over the Chicago home grounds.

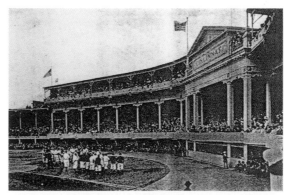

Cincinnati's magnificent new Palace of the Fans opened for business in 1902.

Baltimore Manager John McGraw enflamed the bitter rivalry of the two leagues by deserting the Orioles in mid-season. He took over the New York NL club and took several key players along with him.

1902 (continued)

Three new managers made their 1902 NL debuts in Boston (Buckenberger), Chicago (Sallee) and New York (Fogel—replaced by McGraw in mid season). In the new league, Tom Loftus took over as manager in Washington after Jimmy Manning sold out. Other new managers were Frank Dwyer in Detroit and Bill Armour in Cleveland. The Detroit franchise was in dire straits and was rumored to be relocated to Pittsburgh—another direct threat to the older league. The Cincinnati club showcased their new architectural marvel, the Palace of the Fans. A fine Brooklyn club was mortally wounded at season's end by the defection of Keeler, Kitson, and Donovan to the new league.

Pittsburgh remained unharmed by the player raids and ran away from the pack, winning the NL flag again by 27-1/2 games. The Pirates' Ginger Beaumont led the league at .357 and Jack Chesbro chipped in with 27 victories. Vic Willis fanned 219 batters and Hans Wagner hit .329 with 43 stolen bases.

In the new league, Comiskey's White Stockings yielded the championship to Connie Mack's Athletics, led by Rube Waddell with 24 wins and a league leading 210 strikeouts. Socks Seybold clouted the awesome total of 16 home runs. Boston's Cy Young won 32 games and Washington's Ed Delahanty (in his last full season) was the top batter at .376. Jimmy Callahan of Chicago no-hit the Tigers on September 20.

At year's end, Harry Pulliam of Pittsburgh replaced the threesome of Brush-Soden-Hart as the new president of the National League. The American League had become a fact of life and the end of the costly baseball war was just around the corner.

Veteran Cy Young was caricatured by the Boston newspapers at the 1902 opener at Huntington Avenue.

An All-American League all-star nine played NL champion Pittsburgh in a post-season series, then hooked up with an NL all-star group for a cross-country barnstorming tour in late 1902.

Captain Roy Thomas accepts a floral tribute from the Quaker fans at the 1902 NL opener.

Chicago's Jimmy Callahan blanked the Tigers with no hits at season's end.

Socks Seybold "socked" 16 round-trippers for Connie Mack's Athletics in 1902.

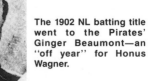

The 1902 NL batting title went to the Pirates' Ginger Beaumont—an "off year" for Honus Wagner.

PITTSBURG AGAIN CLINCHES THE PENNANT BY DEFEATING BROOKLYNS TWICE

CHAMPIONS AGAIN ARE THE PIRATES — TWO GOOD GAMES FROM BROOKLYNS — SAM STRANG GIVES ORIOLES THREE RUNS — OTHER AMATEUR GAMES — LABOR DAY ON THE LOCAL GOLF LINKS

The Pittsburg(h) Dispatch proudly proclaimed the 1902 championship for the Smoky City.

1903

POPE LEO XIII DIES
FIRST PULITZER PRIZES
WRIGHT BROTHERS FLIGHT
FORD MOTOR CO. FORMED
"CALL OF THE WILD" PUBLISHED
"GREAT TRAIN ROBBERY" RELEASED
CURIES WIN NOBEL PRIZE
IROQUOIS THEATER BURNS IN CHICAGO
PAUL GAUGUIN DIES
"PEPSI-COLA" REGISTERED
RELIANCE WINS AMERICA'S CUP
DREYFUS AFFAIR IN FRANCE

In January, peace was restored as a new National agreement recognized the American League. A common body of rules was agreed upon as the newer league accepted the foul strike rule, a controversial item for years to come. Also, as part of the truce accords, the American League agreed to abandon entry in Pittsburgh, assuring Detroit's shaky existence as a big league town. However, the newcomers did announce plans to enter the lucrative New York market by relocating the Baltimore franchise. The all-new New York team secured a plot of ground in upper Manhattan not far from the Polo Grounds, for their field of play.

Also in January, veteran pitcher/utility player Win Mercer committed suicide in San Francisco. Mercer was slated to captain the Detroit team in 1903. A second prominent player death shocked the baseball world in July when star veteran Ed Delahanty, the AL batting champion of the previous season, mysteriously drowned in the Niagara Falls gorge. Tragedy also struck in Philadelphia, where a grandstand section collapsed, killing 14 and injuring many more.

A three-man National Commission was set up to coordinate the dual-league administration and settle all disputes. New NL president Harry Pulliam, AL president Ban Johnson, and new Cincinnati owner Garry Hermann were the principals. John T. Brush of Cincinnati transferred his holdings to become head of the New York Giants. Three new field managers made their debut—Jimmy Callahan with Chicago (AL), Ed Barrow in Detroit, and Chief Zimmer with Philadelphia (NL).

At the NL opening contest in Chicago, Captain Joe Kelly of the Reds prepares to await the first pitch in a seemingly "posed" photograph. The catcher is Johnny Kling and the umpire is Bob Emslie.

Win Mercer, slated to captain and/or manage the Detroit club for 1903, took his own life for reasons unknown.

An artist's report of the unfurling of the 1902 pennant at Philadelphia's Columbia Avenue Park.

Superstar Ed Delahanty perished under mysterious circumstances in the summer of 1903.

Philadelphia and Boston players line up under the balcony of the center field clubhouse at the Phils' home park—part of the opening game rituals.

1903 (continued)

The powerful Pittsburgh Pirates held off McGraw's improved Giant club and won their third straight NL championship. Honus Wagner led the Bucs with his second batting championship, hitting .355. The Giants pitching tandem of McGinnity and Mathewson won 31 and 30 games respectively, with Matty registering 267 strikeouts. Chicago's Frank Chance and Brooklyn's Jimmy Sheckard tied for the stolen base title with 67. The only no-hit game of 1903 was hurled by the Phillies' Chick Fraser on September 18.

The Boston Americans replaced Philadelphia as AL champions with Cy Young, Long Tom Hughes, and Bill Dinneen all contributed 20-plus victories. Buck Freeman contributed 13 HR's and 104 RBI's. Rube Waddell won 22 for the Athletics and whiffed 301 batters. Detroit's newly acquired slugger Sam Crawford celebrated his debut season in the AL with 25 triples and a .332 BA.

With recognition of major league status no longer in question, the pennant-winning Boston Americans challenged the NL champion Pirates to a best-of-nine games post-season series to settle the world's baseball championship. Pittsburgh accepted and the first modern world series was inaugurated. The invincible hurling of Deacon Phillipe provided early victories for the favored Pittsburghs, but Boston closed out the series with four straight victories and fortified the new league's claim as full-fleged major · leaguers. Bill Dinneen and Cy Young were the pitching heroes, winning all five games between them.

In an early 1903 contest at the Athletics' home park, the Highlanders' Ernie Courtney takes his cuts.

Detroit newspaper game-action photo shows Jimmy Barrett roaring into third as Chicago third baseman Isbell awaits the throw. The scene is Bennett Park.

Chick Fraser of the NL Phillies tossed the only no-hitter of 1903.

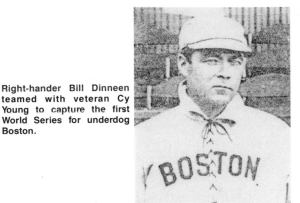

Pirates' hurler Deacon Phillipe was a star performer in a losing cause in the post-season classic.

Right-hander Bill Dinneen teamed with veteran Cy Young to capture the first World Series for underdog Boston.

Boston players, with a large entourage of Beantown's "royal rooters" behind them, pose for the photographer at Pittsburgh during the world's championship games.

After the 1903 World Series was concluded at Boston, the players of both clubs lined up for a combined team photograph—an unheard of display of good sportsmanship considering the bitterness of the preceding years of all-out war.

1904

With all-around attendance on the upswing, both leagues agreed to increase the game schedule from 140 to 154 games. The joint rules committee approved a new balk rule and consented to permit two coaches (at first and third) on the playing field at one time. Several front office changes were in evidence. Rogers and Reach sold controlling interest of the Phillies to James Potter. Bill Yawkey purchased the Detroit club and hired Frank Navin as new secretary/business manager. The Washington franchise was purchased by a new group headed by Tom Noyes and relocated their playing field back to the old NL league park site in north central DC. John Taylor became new-owner of the world champion Boston American League club, replacing Henry Killilea. Buoyed by a resurgence in the standings, the NY Giants made extensive improvements to the Polo Grounds.

Hugh Duffy was hired by the new NL Philadelphia owners to replace Chief Zimmer as manager. Kid Nichols replaced Patsy Donovan in St. Louis and the Cardinals improved their lot, up to fifth place from the 1903 cellar. Malachi Kittridge was the new temporary manager in Washington, but was replaced by Patsy Donovan early in the season. Fielder Jones took over for Jimmy Callahan in Chicago to lead the White Stockings to a third-place finish.

Mgr./Captain Jimmy Collins about to hoist the 1903 championship flag up the centerfield flagpole at the 1904 opening game in Boston.

An interesting 1904 shot of "Matty" delivering to catcher Bowerman at the Polo Grounds. Note the elaborate chalk decorations on the field, the position of the umpire, and the "flat-footed" stance of the catcher.

1904 opening game action at Cleveland shows Chicago's Ducky Holmes scoring the first run of the new season at League Park.

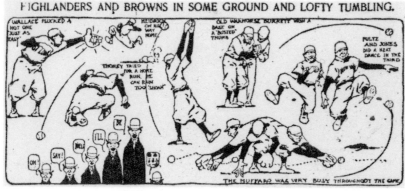

HIGHLANDERS AND BROWNS IN SOME GROUND AND LOFTY TUMBLING.

A NY newspaper cartoonist's comments on a St. Louis/New York game at Hilltop Park.

Brooklyn's Harry Lumley crosses the home plate after homering at New York's Polo Grounds. The Giants' catcher is Jack Warner.

1904 (continued)

1904 was truly a season of extraordinary pitching. On May 5, Boston's Cy Young tossed a perfect game, one of his 26 victories of the season. Jack Chesbro of the New York Americans turned in a Herculean performance, winning 41 games—almost enough to single-handedly deliver a pennant to Manhattan. The eccentric one, Rube Waddell of the Athletics, fanned a total of 349 batters, piling up 26 victories in the process. Cleveland's Addie Joss was the stingiest of all AL pitchers, registering a 1.59 ERA. Over in the National League, the duo of Mathewson and McGinnity provided 33 and 35 victories for McGraw's pennant-winning New York Giants, who piled up 106 wins and outdistanced runner-up Chicago by 13 games.

The Boston Americans repeated as pennant winners, nosing out a surprising New York Highlander club at the very end. NY hurler Jack Chesbro tarnished his magnificent iron-man season by permitting the pennant winning run to Boston via a wild pitch. Veteran Willie Keeler paced the New York hitting attack with a .343 average. Cleveland's Nap Lajoie won the league batting championship, his second straight, at .381. Honus Wagner likewise repeated as NL hitting champ with a .349 average, also stealing 53 bases to lead the majors. Almost lost in the myriad of pitching feats of 1904 was a June 11 no-hitter by the Cubs' Bob Wicker.

The defending world champion Boston club once again challenged the NL champion Giants to a post-season showdown, but the New Yorkers declined. Partly motivated by John McGraw's bitterness toward Ban Johnson and the new league, the Giants arrogantly claimed the world championship was already theirs and they were not obligated to risk it in an abbreviated playoff. Their stubborn stance ultimately backfired on them in the court of public opinion and the following year the Fall Classic was permanently resumed.

The Boston Globe hails a second straight pennant by Jimmy Collins' crew, but no world championship since McGraw's Giants refused to participate.

Rube Waddell of the Athletics had his finest season, with 26 wins and a record total of 349 strikeouts.

NY Highlander hurler Jack Chesbro amassed 41 victories in 1904, only to lose the AL flag to Boston on a wild pitch at season's end.

The AL pennant struggle was a classic between the Bostons and New Yorks. Boston's Freddie Parent is shown at bat in a crucial October game with the Highlanders at Huntington Avenue Grounds.

Veteran Cy Young registered a perfect game against the Athletics en route to his 26 victories in 1904.

1905

NON-BASEBALL NEWS EVENTS OF 1905

RIOTS IN PETROGRAD
IWW ORGANIZED IN CHICAGO
TREATY OF PORTSMOUTH ENDS RUSSO-JAPANESE WAR
EINSTEIN PROPOSES THEORY OF RELATIVITY
ROOSEVELT INVESTIGATES STANDARD OIL TRUST
PEARY SAILS FOR NORTH POLE
JULES VERNE DIES
FIRST DIODE RADIO TUBE
AMUNDSEN FINDS NORTH POLE
FOOTBALL REFORMS PASSED

A couple of new team nicknames were in the news early in 1905. The Cleveland club, tiring of the name "BLUES," adopted NAPOLEONS, or NAPS, in honor of their current star and new manager Napoleon Lajoie. Washington, despite the obvious confusion of the same name used by several teams in the National League, declared the name SENATORS defunct and re-christened themselves NATIONALS. The National League signed on a new umpire named Bill Klem. Also worth noting was the arrival of young outfielder Tyrus Cobb on the Detroit roster in August.

Besides Lajoie in Cleveland, new faces abounded in the managerial ranks. In the American League, Jake Stahl became the fifth Washington manager in as many years while Bill Armour took the reins in Detroit. In the NL, long-time local favorite Fred Tenney was Boston's new man at the helm and the equally popular Frank Chance of the Cubs replaced ailing Frank Selee in mid-season. The St. Louis Cardinals floundered after hastily replacing departed manager Kid Nichols with, first, Jimmy Burke, and then part-owner Stanley Robison.

Another pennant is hoisted up the Huntington Avenue flagpole in April 1905. Captains Jimmy Collins and Lave Cross of the Athletics do the honors.

Boston's Vic Willis established a decade low with 29 losses in 1905. In spite of this he was one of the finest hurlers of his era, winning 183 games from 1900-1909 with two NL teams.

A wild 18-year-old kid named Cobb was picked up by the Detroit club from Augusta in late 1905.

In 1905 action at Cincinnati, the Giants' Mike Donlin is rounding third only to see that the third out was made. Rookie Al Bridwell is the Reds' third baseman.

A Chicago newspaper cartoon laments the overweight appearance of the hometown White Stockings.

1905 (continued)

It was another season of good pitching, especially in the American League where there were no less than ten 20-game winners and a league leading batting average of only .306 (Elmer Flick). With exceptionally strong starting rotations (Waddell, Plank, Bender & Coakley), the Athletics edged out the Chicago White Sox (Owen, Altrock, Smith & White) for the AL flag. The combined ERA of both staffs was close to 2.00, remarkably low as a team standard. Four no-hit games in the major leagues were registered by the following: Christy Mathewson, Weldon Henley, Frank Smith, and Bill Dinneen. Mathewson recorded his third straight 30-plus game winning season, firmly establishing himself as the top hurler in the NL. McGinnity and Ames chipped in with 22 wins each as the Giants coasted to their second straight pennant under fiery John McGraw. Cincinnati's Cy Seymour wrested the batting championship from Wagner with a .377 average to go along with 219 hits, 40 doubles and 21 stolen bases. Wagner made a race of it with a .363 final BA.

The talent-laden Giants, with 106 victories, this time confidently accepted the AL challenge for a post-season series to decide the "world" championship. With new procedures for future series now formulated, a best-of-seven format was adopted. McGraw, always the innovative competitor and with the extra time allowed by an early clinch, ordered special black uniforms for his Giants. The black-clad New Yorkers prevailed over Mack's "White Elephants" 4 games to 1 with Mathewson contributing three shut-outs. The other Giant victory was also a whitewash by McGinnity, as was the lone Philadelphia win by Chief Bender. The triumph only underscored McGraw's cocky, defiant conviction that he had the finest team in the "superior" National League. Despite the association and identification with successful conquest, the black uniforms received general disfavor and some ridicule even with New Yorkers.

Rookie umpire Bill Klem made his NL debut in 1905.

Pitcher-turned-outfielder Cy Seymour of Cincinnati won batting honors in the senior circuit with a lusty .377 mark.

Chief Bender chipped in with a shutout victory, the only win for Connie Mack's club in the Fall Classic.

Joe McGinnity tossed one of the five all-shutout games in the 1905 World Championship series.

Christy Mathewson had his finest hour in the 1905 World Series, winning three games, all shutouts. He's pictured here in the New Yorkers' controversial all-black uniform.

A panoramic view of the vast throng at the second game of the 1905 championship series at New York's Polo Grounds. The locale is the left field corner.

1906

The baseball world was saddened in late March by the death from malaria of young Washington shortstop Joe Cassidy. John McGraw, still gloating over his series victory, ordered new uniforms with "WORLD'S CHAMPIONS" emblazoned on the shirt fronts of both home and away games. The flip side of this tasteless display of team pride was the plight of the cellar-dwelling St. Louis Browns of the AL. Hoping an abandonment of the BROWNS identification might bring better luck, they presented radically redesigned black-trimmed uniforms and a new nickname— RAVENS. Perhaps it worked as the new RAVENS climbed up to 5th place in the standings, only. two games removed from the lofty first division. Another new umpire named Billy Evans made his AL debut in 1906. The Athletics also introduced a promising recruit named Eddie Collins that year.

In Philadelphia, former Phillie field manager Bill Shettsline was named club president. Also, Charles Murphy, the one-time baseball scribe, assumed the presidency of the Chicago Cubs. For the Cubs, 1906 was to be a year of destiny—a destiny of mixed blessings. They literally destroyed McGraw's vision of New York supremacy by winning a record total of 116 games (a .763 percentage)—a full 20 games ahead of the Giants, whose 96 wins would have won the championship in other years. The dark side of the Cubs' destiny would soon follow in the post-season classic.

Superbas Manager Ned Hanlon was hired to lead the Cincinnati Reds for 1906 and was replaced in Brooklyn by veteran Patsy Donovan. The St. Louis Cardinals settled on Jack McCloskey as their new field boss. Popular Jimmy Collins, tired of the strain of managing, yielded the reins of the Boston Americans to Chick Stahl at season's end. The once mighty Bostons, cursed by anemic batting and disastrous seasons for Cy Young (13-21) and Bill Dinneen (8-19), settled into the AL basement solidified by a 20-game losing streak.

Promising infielder Joe Cassidy of the Washington club expired unexpectedly in the spring of 1906.

Umpire Billy Evans joined the AL crew in 1906.

Giants' Manager John McGraw confers with Phils' Pilot Hugh Duffy before the 1906 opener. As his uniform indicates, the New Yorkers were not humble about their convincing World Series victory in 1905.

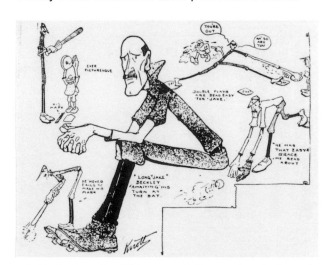

A St. Louis cartoonist lampooned the angular physique of Cardinals' veteran first baseman Jake Beckley.

At Philadelphia's Columbia Avenue Park, the 1905 pennant is raised at the home opener. Philadelphia's Mayor Weaver, on the far left, supervises the effort.

1906 (continued)

The White Sox, on the strength of a late season 19-game winning streak, prevailed as AL champions, setting the stage for an all-Chicago world championship series. Fielder Jones' "hitless wonders" batted .230 as a team and hit a team total of six home runs—six less than the Athletics' Harry Davis hit by himself. However, their pitching rotation of Frank Owen, Nick Altrock, Doc White, and Ed Walsh was peerless. White finished with an ERA of 1.52 and Walsh contributed 10 shut-outs. George Stone of St. Louis edged out Nap Lajoie for the batting crown .358 to .355, while the 19-year old Cobb hit a respectable .316 for the 6th place Tigers. New York's Al Orth topped the AL with 27 victories. In September, the hapless Boston Americans and the Philadelphia A's made history by playing 24 innings, almost three games-in-one.

In the senior circuit, Honus Wagner reclaimed the batting title with .339 and Christy Mathewson "slumped" to 22 victories. As to be expected, the Cubs, or "Giant Killers" as one Chicago newspaper coined them, produced the premier pitching staff paced by Mordecai "Three-Finger" Brown's 26 victories. John Lush of the Phillies recorded a no-hit game on May 1 while Brooklyn hurlers Mal Eason and Harry McIntyre duplicated the feat within 12 days of each other.

The city of Chicago was delirious in October as the local teams vied for the baseball championship of the world. The heavily favored Cubs were upset by the lowly Southsiders 4 games to 2 as an obscure utility infielder named George Rohe (.258 season BA) provided winning hits in two games. As the invincible Cubs would demonstrate in subsequent Fall Classics, it was one of the greatest upsets in the history of post-season play. The two Chicago teams would never again meet for the world title, so the results remain forever unavenged.

A popular two-way button was worn by many Chicago fans in October 1906.

Pitcher Gus Dorner of the Boston Nationals had the dubious distinction of losing 26 games.

Journeyman infielder George Rohe of Comiskey's club was an unlikely hero in the series.

A group of Comiskey's "hitless wonders" (L to R: Isbell, Rohe, Jones, Donahue, Towne, and Walsh) pose for the camera at the Cubs' West Side Grounds.

George Stone of the AL St. Louis club was the league's leading batsman in 1906 with a .358 BA. He's shown here crossing home plate in a game against Cleveland.

Chicago newspapers enjoyed a rare baseball bonanza—a "once in a lifetime" for Windy City baseball fans.

White Sox catcher Billy Sullivan at bat in one of the games at Cubs' park. The catcher is Kling and the umpire is Johnstone.

1907

NON-BASEBALL
NEWS EVENTS
OF 1907

GREAT WHITE FLEET SAILS
STATEHOOD FOR OKLAHOMA
KIPLING WINS NOBEL PRIZE
HARRY THAW ON TRIAL
PEKING-PARIS AUTO RACE
LUSITANIA'S MAIDEN VOYAGE
GIBSON GIRL THE RAGE
BIG BILL HAYWOOD TRIAL
ZIEGFELD FOLLIES BEGUN
BADEN-POWELL ORGANIZES BOY SCOUTS
KETCHELL WINS TITLE
MAURETANIA SETS RECORD

In January, the Boston NL franchise was purchased by George Dovey and one of his first dictates was a totally new uniform design, replacing the familiar red stockings and trim. The new home suits featured an all-white appearance, including the stockings. Observers were quick to re-christen the club "DOVES" after the new owner and the new uniforms. The road suits also attracted attention since they were made from a gray flannel fabric that embodied a pattern of vertical green stripes. This idea would evolve into a more pronounced "pin-stripe" look that flourished in the following decade. Double tragedy struck Boston in late March with the death of Doves' outfielder Cozy Dolan, only the day after Boston AL player/manager Chick Stahl committed suicide. Stahl's death was demoralizing to the Boston Americans and they struggled through the season with a succession of interim managers, finally settling on Deacon McGuire as field boss.

The Brooklyn road uniforms were even more conspicuous than those of the Doves, made from a gray fabric with a blue "checked" stripe pattern. Giants backstop Roger Bresnahan introduced "cricket-style" shin guards when the season opened but it would take many more seasons before this item became standard gear for catchers.

New field managers for 1907 included Billy Murray (replacing Hugh Duffy) of the Philadelphia Nationals, Joe Cantillon (replacing Jake Stahl) at Washington, and Hugh Jennings (replacing Bill Armour) in Detroit. Among the new AL players in 1907 were Washington pitcher Walter Johnson and Boston outfielder Tris Speaker. Cy Young bounced back from an off year, winning 22 while Addie Joss and Doc White won 27 each.

The star shortstop of the Browns, Bobby Wallace, is shown "legging out" a grounder in a 1907 game in St. Louis' Sportsman's Park. The world champion Chicago White Sox are the opponents.

OPENING DAY DREAMS.

The Brooklyn Eagle's cartoonist expresses the eternal optimism of baseball fandom in the spring. Unfortunately, 1907 provided another second division finish for manager Patsy Donovan.

Chick Stahl, the Boston Americans' new player/-manager, took his own life in March 1907.

Boston baseball fans were further devastated by the demise of Doves' outfielder Cozy Dolan, only a day after Stahl's suicide.

1907 (continued)

Excitement was high in Detroit as new manager Hugh "Eeh-Yah" Jennings prodded the Tigers into a first-place finish. Young outfielder Ty Cobb came into his own with a league-leading .350 BA to go along with 116 RBI's and 49 stolen bases. Sam Crawford chipped in with .323 and the pitching staff of Donovan, Killian, Mullin and Siever accounted for 89 of the club's 92 victories. Anticipating good crowds for the final pennant drive and a post-season series, Bennett Park was enlarged in August by pushing back the right field fence and building a huge new bleacher section. As a reward for the team's successes, Secretary Navin was allowed to purchase controlling interest of the club at year's end.

In the senior circuit, Hans Wagner won another batting title (.350). Two no-hit games were pitched in the National League—on May 8, by Big Jeff Pfeffer of Boston and on September 20 by Nick Maddox of the Pirates. The powerful Cubs easily captured the flag again paced by Orval Overall (23 wins) and Mordecai Brown (20 wins). The Chicagoans were clearly the "class" of major league baseball as they vindicated themselves in the world championship series, crushing the Tigers in a four-game sweep. The sensational youngster Cobb was virtually impotent in the series, with only four hits off Cub pitching. Cub catcher Johnny Kling was superlative in gunning down Cobb and other Tigers on the basepaths.

Giants' catcher Roger Bresnahan revolutionized the fine art of back-stopping with the wearing of protective shin guards in 1907.

A 19-year-old pitching wonder from Kansas, one Walter Johnson, made his ML debut with the hapless Washington club in 1907.

The official scorecard for the 1907 World Series, available for the price of one thin dime.

Late in the 1907 season the Detroit club, destined to face the powerful Chicago NL club in post-season play, were tormented with the strains of the Illinois fight song by Chicago fans on their last visit to the Windy City. In response, Hugh Jennings is shown leading his Tiger "choir" in a rousing chorus of Michigan's "Hail to the Victors" for the benefit of the White Sox fans.

In the series opener at Chicago, Detroit's Germany Schaefer (on ground) is run down between home and third. Frank Chance is guarding home plate on the left, Steinfeldt is about to make the tag, and pitcher Overall is standing on the right. The game ended in a tie.

A Baseball Magazine cartoon "rubs it in" to Tiger fans after their one-sided defeat at the hands of the Cubs.

1908

Makeshift press accommodations on the pavilion roof at Bennett Park during the 1907 series were so repugnant to the visiting reporters that they banded together to assure, among other matters, that their needs would be better satisfied by club owners henceforth. Thus the Baseball Writers Association of America (BBWAA) was formed over the winter of 1907-08. In Boston, the first issue of BASEBALL magazine was published. Steadily increasing attendance spurred significant park improvements and enlargements in several cities—notably for the Cubs, Tigers, Brooklyn and both Boston facilities. Connie Mack finally gave up on his unruly pitcher Rube Waddell and sold him to the St. Louis American League club, but he had high hopes for newcomer Joe Jackson, the "shoeless" one.

New field managers were signed on for Cincinnati (John Ganzell) and for the Boston Nationals (Joe Kelley). Kid Elberfield relieved Clark Griffith as manager of the NY Highlanders, who plummeted to the AL cellar with 103 losses. Later in the season, Fred Lake relieved Boston AL manager McGuire. The home town fans paid tribute with special days for a pair of ML superstars, Honus Wagner and Cy Young, during the 1908 season. Wagner was honored in Pittsburgh on July 18 and Cy Young in Boston on August 13. Maverick first baseman Hal Chase of the Highlanders "jumped ship" and joined an outlaw team in California.

Detroit scribe Joe Jackson was named president of the newly formed Baseball Writers Association of America.

In a 1908 game at Washington, Captain Bob Ganley is shown attempting to steal third base.

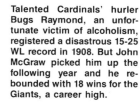 

Talented Cardinals' hurler Bugs Raymond, an unfortunate victim of alcoholism, registered a disastrous 15-25 WL record in 1908. But John McGraw picked him up the following year and he rebounded with 18 wins for the Giants, a career high.

Another popular veteran, Cy Young, had a big special day of tribute by Boston fans in August 1908. He is seen here receiving a loving cup from visiting White Sox pilot Fielder Jones. Captain Jake Stahl is on the right.

The popular native of nearby Carnegie, superstar Honus Wagner, was honored with a special day at Exposition Park.

1908 (continued)

It was another banner year for pitchers with six no-hitters, two in the NL and four in the AL. On October 2, Addie Joss of Cleveland made history with a perfect game, beating Chicago's Ed Walsh 1-0. A pity for Walsh, since he fanned 15 in a losing cause but the White Sox hurler managed to win 40 other games during the season, compiling a 1.42 ERA in the process. Waddell won 19 for his new team, the Browns, and helped elevate them into the first division. Detroit's Ed Summers won 24 as the Tigers nipped Cleveland for their second straight pennant. Cobb repeated as batting champ, an event that was to become an annual habit for the Georgian.

In the National League, Christy Mathewson led all hurlers with 37 victories and a 1.43 ERA. The Cubs Mordecai Brown wasn't far behind with 29 wins and a 1.47 ERA. In a sad note, alcoholism began to take its toll on Cardinals pitcher Bugs Raymond, who managed to lose 25 games. Wagner of Pittsburgh was once again the top batsman with .354 plus 101 RBI's and 53 stolen bases. The Cubs repeated as pennant winners but it required a post-season playoff contest with the Giants at the Polo Grounds on October 8 to settle the issue. The playoff was necessitated by the famous Merkle "Boner" two weeks earlier and it matched up the two top hurlers of the league, Mathewson and Brown. Mordecai proved to be the master on this historic occasion, beating Matty 4-2.

After such dramatic finishes in both leagues, the World Series was strictly anticlimatic with the Cubs once again subduing the Detroit club with ease, 4 games to 1. Ty Cobb hit a more respectable .368 in the series and George Mullin avoided a sweep with a strong pitching performance in game 3, but Brown and Orval Overall were untouchable, winning two games each to seal the victory. Chicago's West Side was the undisputed home of baseball's elite.

Future Hall-of-Famer Ed Walsh enjoyed his finest season, with 40 wins and an incredible 1.42 ERA.

Cleveland's brilliant Addie Joss hurled perfection in October 1908 vs. the Chicago White Sox and Ed Walsh.

Hal Chase, the fielding marvel of the New York Americans, made news in 1908 by deserting his contract. It was another maneuver that only added to his reputation as a career malcontent.

The Giants' Fred Merkle, a fine all-around player, made an unfortunate careless mistake in a crucial game that forever cursed an otherwise standout career.

Tiger pitcher George Mullin, an outstanding hitter, is shown on base in the '08 series. He was the winning hurler in the only Detroit victory in the Fall Classic.

Game action in the 1908 championship series between Cubs and Tigers. A frustrated Ty Cobb is tagged out at the plate by catcher Johnny Kling. Chicago prevailed with ease, 4 games to 1.

1909

PEARY REACHES NORTH POLE

ROOSEVELT ON SAFARI

GERONIMO DIES

BARNEY OLDFIELD SETS
AUTO SPEED RECORD

WORLDS FAIR IN SEATTLE

ENGLISH CHANNEL CROSSED
BY AIRPLANE

PEARY/COOK DISPUTE OVER
NORTH POLE

GORE WINS WIMBLEDON

GLENN CURTIS WINS AVIATION CUP

MARCONI WINS NOBEL PRIZE

KETCHELL/JOHNSON FIGHT

The 1909 season marked the beginning of the era of all concrete-and-steel baseball parks. Wooden stands in three major league cities were replaced by "fireproof" double-decked grandstands. In St. Louis, the Browns (RAVENS never seemed to catch on) retained their old wooden grandstand as a left field corner pavilion and re-oriented the diamond 90 degrees to accommodate their spacious new structure. Completely new facilities on new sites were the case in Philadelphia (Shibe Park) and Pittsburgh (Forbes Field). Similar new structures surfaced annually for the next five years around the major league cities.

A host of new field managers were also showcased as the season opened: Clark Griffith at Cincinnati, Roger Bresnahan at St. Louis (NL), Frank Bowerman at Boston (NL), Harry Lumley at Brooklyn. In the AL, George Stallings at New York, Billy Sullivan at Chicago and Jim McGuire at Cleveland (a carry-over from late 1908) were the newcomers.

Tragedy struck the Athletics as catcher Mike Powers succumbed to gangrene poisoning and died on April 26. But the National League was jolted by a double dose of grim news as president Harry Pulliam, after suffering a severe nervous breakdown earlier in the year, committed suicide on July 29. John Heydler assumed the league presidency on an interim basis and ended up with the position on a permanent basis. At year's end, two more major league players were felled by Bright's disease—pitcher Bill Hogg and outfielder Jimmy Sebring.

The tragic death of Mike "Doc" Powers was shocking news to Connie Mack's Athletics.

Powers' Athletics teammates acted as pallbearers. From left to right: Simon Nicholls, Danny Murphy, Eddie Plank, Harry Davis, Ira Thomas, and Jack Coombs.

Former Boston battery mates Cy Young and Lou Criger, now with Cleveland and St. Louis, greet each other at the brand new Sportsman's Park inauguration.

Philadelphia fans converge on the magnificent new home of the Athletics, Shibe Park, just prior to the grand opening in April 1909.

NL President Harry Pulliam took his own life in the summer of 1909, sending shock waves through the baseball world.

An experimental night game took place between some local teams at Cincinnati's Palace of the Fans in June 1909.

1909 (continued)

Red Ames of the Giants had the rare misfortune of hurling a no-hit game for nine innings only to lose it in the 13th to Brooklyn on April 15. On June 18, a novel experiment was conducted at Cincinnati's Palace of the Fans. Arc lights were installed around the park and a trial night baseball game was played (not involving the Reds). The results were less than spectacular and the idea was shelved as an unworkable scheme for major league baseball. A month later in Cleveland, the Naps' second baseman Neil Ball executed a rare unassisted triple play in a game against Boston.

In the pennant races, Detroit won its third straight AL flag under Hugh Jennings, edging out Mack's Athletics, a team at the brink of a dynasty. Ty Cobb had his greatest season yet, winning a triple crown (.377 BA, 115 RBI, & 9 HR). Crawford hit .314 and led the league in doubles with 35. George Mullin had a career-high club record with 29 victories and Ed Willett followed with 22. The White Sox once-mighty pitching rotation was unable to overcome a .221 team batting average, with only Frank Smith cashing in 25 wins.

Despite another 100-plus wins by the talented Cubs, Pittsburgh put it all together in 1909 with 110 victories and a six-game bulge over Chicago. Wagner won his fourth straight batting crown (.339) and pitchers Howie Camnitz and Vic Willis provided 25 and 22 wins respectively. Young Babe Adams contributed with a dozen wins and saved his best for the post-season showdown with Detroit.

The Tigers finally made a competitive bid to capture the World Championship but were unable to solve the slants of Pirate pitcher Adams. The Babe was the hero of the hour for the Pirates, winning three times. The much ballyhooed confrontation between superstars Cobb and Wagner easily went to the Dutchman. Neither player would ever appear again in a Fall Classic.

Leon "Red" Ames of New York no-hit Brooklyn and ended up losing in extra innings.

Detroit's premier moundsman George Mullin won 29 games for the pennant winners and then won two World Series contests in a losing cause.

Pittsburgh's new Forbes Field grandstand was packed with humanity for the post-season classic vs. Detroit.

Cleveland second baseman Neil Ball performed an unassisted triple play, then posed with his three Boston victims.

1909 World Series action in Detroit. The Tigers' Jim Delahanty is caught in a rundown between third and home. Pirates' catcher George Gibson is making the tag.

Charles "Babe" Adams, a 12-game winner during the season, was untouchable in the series. He won three of the four Pirate victories.

The top batsmen in their respective leagues, Cobb and Wagner, were the focus of media attention during the 1909 World Series.